The Search for Christian America

The Search For Christian America

Mark A. Noll
Nathan O. Hatch
George M. Marsden

CROSSWAY BOOKS • WESTCHESTER ILLINOIS
A DIVISION OF GOOD NEWS PUBLISHERS

The Search for Christian America © 1983 by Mark A. Noll, Nathan O.
Hatch and George M. Marsden. Published by Crossway Books, a division
of Good News Publishers, 9825 West Roosevelt Road, Westchester, Illinois
60153.

First printing 1983

Printed in the United States of America

Library of Congress Catalog Card Number 83-71239

ISBN 0-89107-285-3

To Mary and David Noll
Gregg and David Hatch
Greg and Brynn Marsden

Contents

Acknowledgments and Credits

Chapters 1, 3, 5, 6, 7, and 8, with the exception of brief parts of Chapters 1 and 5, as noted below, were prepared expressly for this volume. Much of the material in these chapters, however, is the product of more specialized research from which the authors have also drawn material for academic books and articles. Reference to that more specialized writing is found in notes to the various chapters.

About three pages in Chapter 1 and twelve paragraphs in Chapter 5 are revised from pages 207-210, 214-218, and 222-224 of *The Gospel in America* by John D. Woodbridge, Mark A. Noll and Nathan O. Hatch, copyright © 1979 by John D. Woodbridge, Mark A. Noll and Nathan O. Hatch. Used by permission of the Zondervan Corporation.

Chapter 2 is revised from *John Calvin: His Influence in the Western World*, edited by W. Stanford Reid, copyright © 1982 by the Zondervan Corporation. Used by permission.

Roughly 30 percent of Chapter 4 represents a completely rewritten presentation of parts of an essay on "The Bible in Revolutionary America" prepared by Mark Noll for publication in *The Bible in American Law, Politics and Rhetoric*, edited by James T. Johnson (Fortress Press and Scholars Press, 1983). The helpful assistance of Prof. Johnson is gratefully acknowledged.

An abridged and earlier version of Chapter 6 has appeared as "Quest for a Christian America" by George Marsden, in the May 1983 issue of *Eternity*. The assistance of *Eternity's* executive editor, Stephen Board, is gratefully acknowledged.

Biblical quotations are from *The Holy Bible: New International Version*, copyright 1978 by New York International Bible Society, published by the Zondervan Corporation, Grand Rapids, Michigan.

The book is a joint product of the thinking of Nathan Hatch, George Marsden, and Mark Noll, who for many years have been doing research, exchanging papers, and talking together about concerns reflected in this book. Nathan Hatch provided the drafts of Chapters 5 and 7, George Marsden of Chapters 2 and 6, and Mark Noll of Chapters 1, 3, and 4. All contributed to the process of revision which was under the general oversight of Mark Noll. Randall Balmer graciously took time from his doctoral program in the History of Christianity at Princeton University to prepare the bibliographical essay.

During the course of its preparation this book has benefited from an exchange of correspondence with Francis and Franky Schaeffer. The Schaeffers will not agree with everything here, but they should realize that their points of view have been listened to with care.

Further thanks are due to Mark R. Amstutz and Richard J. Mouw for suggestions concerning part four of the bibliographical essay, to C. T. McIntire and Harry S. Stout for helpful comments to George Marsden on an earlier draft of Chapter 2, and to Mrs. Anne Edgin of Juniata College for her efficient typing and manifest good sense. Julie Hatch, Lucie Marsden, and Maggie Noll deserve better than to be married to historians, but they put up with it remarkably well. Jan Dennis and Lane Dennis of Crossway Books have been exemplary editors who have gone well beyond the normal call of duty in their assistance to the project.

CHAPTER ONE

The Search for Christian America:
Introduction

At times of crisis it is a natural human reaction to turn to the past for support. Evangelicals and fundamentalists in modern America are no different. We have suffered with the nation through the traumas of Vietnam and Watergate. And we continue to share fully in the uncertainties of a ricocheting economy and nuclear-shrouded international tensions. But as theologically conservative Christians, evangelicals and fundamentalists are troubled by another dimension of modern American life: its flight from morality and godliness. The collapse of discipline in the schools, the spread of pornography, the strident voices proclaiming "rights" for homosexuals and "freedom" for abortion, along with the manifest presence of great social injustices, fill us with foreboding. To resist the evil of our day and to build a healthier society we almost instinctively turn to those who have gone before for wisdom and practical guidance. At stake is nothing less than what was once widely assumed to be America's Christian heritage.

EVANGELICAL MOBILIZATION

It is undeniable that American evangelicals in recent years have taken a more fervent interest in public life. Prominent leaders are speaking out forcefully on issues of government policy like defense and questions of national morality like abortion. Voters concerned about moral issues, often urged on by political action committees with ties to evangelicals, have made their presence felt in elections. They may have played a role in the election of Ronald Reagan as president in 1980. They certainly have helped to defeat certain candidates in local and state elections.

Two recent events seem to have stimulated this renewed evangelical involvement in the public sphere. The first was the ruling of the Supreme Court on abortion in 1973. Its decision in *Roe v. Wade*, which in effect legalized abortion-on-demand, angered many evangelicals. That decision sparked active political involvement. And it has led to repeated calls for defense of Judeo-Christian reverence for life.

The second event was the nation's Bicentennial in 1976. During that year evangelical publishers turned out an array of nationalistic titles, such as *America: God Shed His Grace on Thee; One Nation Under God;* and *Faith, Stars and Stripes.* A host of evangelical magazines extolled America's Christian heritage, the biblical origins of American government, and the spiritual insights of the founding fathers. "America," suggested one in typical fashion, "has a great past, a great present, and a great future, because America has a GREAT GOD."

During the Bicentennial celebrations other leaders evoked powerful religious images concerning the American past, like George Washington kneeling before God at Valley Forge or Benjamin Franklin breaking a deadlock at the Constitutional Convention by calling for prayer. Some speakers also pointed to the central role of Scripture in the creation of the United States. Said one at a "Festival of Faith": "The men who signed the Declaration of Independence were moved by a magnificent dream. . . . And this dream is rooted in the book we call the Bible."[1]

The combination of these two events—the shocking decision of the Supreme Court on abortion and the Bicentennial reminder of the Christian past—led to a new evangelical engagement in public life and fueled actions that were already underway.[2] Protests against abortion-on-demand, opposition to the Equal Rights Amendment, public appeals to save the family, campaigns against pornography, protests against the removal of prayer from public schools, and appeals for national military strength against godless foreign foes have become well-established parts of American evangelical culture.

In addition, several groups with evangelical connections have mounted campaigns with more positive goals. Evangelicals have helped found homes for mothers to bear babies who otherwise might have been aborted, they have taken part in efforts to make the nation's prisons more humane, and they have aided efforts to feed the world's hungry.

Much of the evangelical concern about public life has risen in response to the perception of a spreading "secular humanism." This world view, which to some is the product of a well-organized conspiracy and to others a more general cultural trend, rules God out of the picture, sees the world only in material terms, abandons theistic foundations for traditional freedoms, and treats religion as an illusion. The fight against this secular humanism has been carried into school boards, the courts, and legislative assemblies.

A VISION OF THE PAST

An important part of this concern about "secular humanism" is historical. Many evangelical leaders regard it as a relatively new intrusion into American life. The adoption and influence of secular humanism is seen as a momentous new development in American history. It is said to represent nothing less than the triumph of atheism and irreligion over the Christian heritage of America.

It follows, then, that one of the calls to reform America in our day becomes an appeal to recover the Christian roots, the Christian heritage, the Christian values of an older America. Our instinctive reaction is to regain what we have lost. To make such a recovery, it is thought, would put modern evangelicals in a place once again to encourage righteousness in the land and overcome the evils of our society.

This view of the past is the one which featured so prominently in celebrations of the Bicentennial. It is one which makes much of the piety of the Pilgrims and of the Puritans. It is one which regards the great revivals of earlier American history as crucial shapers of our culture. And, above all, it is a view which holds the American Revolution and the creation of a new United States in special reverence. The new nation, it is widely felt, emerged from the generally Christian actions of generally Christian people. And these actions bequeathed Christian values, and a Christian heritage, to later American history. But now recent national backsliding has placed that entire Christian heritage in jeopardy.

Such widespread public opinions about the United States' Christian past are, very naturally, of great interest to historians of America who are also Christians. The authors of this book belong to that number. We earn our daily bread by teaching about the past, we regularly read the work of other practitioners in the field, and we spend considerable time in libraries and archives doing our own research. But we are also evangelical Christians who are concerned about the fate of the church in twentieth-century America. We feel, therefore, that we have a special stake in discovering how the activity of Christians shaped the country. It is not surprising that we are very much concerned with the question of whether America's past was really Christian or not.

All three of us have addressed the question of America's Christian character in more technical or specialized studies.[3] We have written for our academic peers about individual Christians, churches, and larger Christian groups from various eras in the nation's history. And for such audiences we have also dealt with questions concerning the way Christianity has influenced American life and how American life has influenced the Christians. We have also tried to share some of the insights of our historical work more broadly by writing popular books and articles for Christian magazines and publishers.[4] Each of us would be pleased for any who are intrigued or disturbed by the conclusions of this book to refer to the other things we have written for a closer look at the research on which this volume's arguments rest. Even more, we would be pleased to have our conclusions checked against other solid studies of American history, such as those mentioned in the bibliographical essay or those available in any good library.

At the present, however, it has seemed useful for us to combine our efforts in order to make a careful search for Christian America. Our purpose is to examine carefully the popular belief that America was once a "Christian nation" which has now been all but overrun by secular humanism. To put it most simply: is this a factual picture, a mythical picture, or something else altogether?

THE ARGUMENT OF THE BOOK

We have three general concerns in making this inquiry. The first has to do with the accuracy of our picture of the past. We wish to report as simply as possible what actually happened in early America, with particular reference to the activities and aspirations of Christians. But, secondly, we want to go beyond a concern for setting the historical record straight by also asking how a proper understanding of Scripture should influence our thoughts about the nation. To accomplish this goal it will be necessary to pose careful questions about what we mean when we talk about "a Christian country" and "a Christian heritage." Thirdly, we feel that the historical and theoretical discussion involved in addressing our first two concerns leads to important practical implications. How we regard the past often dramatically shapes our perception of the present. And so we hope that this book about history will leave some positive suggestions about how Christians may responsibly use the past in acting for Christ in the world today.

The argument of this book can be stated quite simply.

1) We feel that a careful study of the facts of history shows that early America does not deserve to be considered uniquely, distinctly or even predominately Christian, if we mean by the word "Christian" a state of society reflecting the ideals presented in Scripture. There is no lost golden age to which American Christians may return. In addition, a careful study of history will also show that evangelicals themselves were often partly to blame for the spread of secularism in contemporary American life.

2) We feel also that careful examination of Christian teaching on government, the state, and the nature of culture shows that the idea of a "Christian nation" is a very ambiguous concept which is usually harmful to effective Christian action in society.

The chapters of this book provide evidence for this twofold thesis. Some of them, particularly the early ones, take a hard look at the Christian character of crucial groups, issues, and events in the early history of English-speaking North America. Others, particularly those in the second half of the book, consider more directly contemporary versions of the effort to describe an American Christian past. They also address more specifically the ways in which Christians may use historical insight to strengthen both belief and practice in the present. As the chapters unfold it will become apparent that we are not approaching this inquiry in a heavy-handed or spiteful manner. In fact, one of our auxiliary purposes is to show that Christians in the history of America have often displayed a genuine and sincere faith, and that this faith has played an important role in American history.

STRIKING A BALANCE

In making our case, we do not want to contend that Christian values have been absent from American history. On the contrary, we hope to show that there has been much commendable Christian belief, practice, and influence in the history of the United States and the colonies which formed the new country. Christian goals and aspirations certainly had a part in the settlement of North America. It is also indubitable that Christian factors contributed to the struggle for national independence and that Christian principles played a role in the founding documents of the United States. We want to give due recognition to these positive Christian aspects of our history, for they have had a marked influence on the shape of modern America. Their presence, we agree, justifies a picture of the United States as a singularly *religious* country.

Recent polls in America and Western Europe underscore the continuing strength of this religious heritage. Surveys by the Gallup Organization in 1981 revealed that over 40 percent of America's population was likely to attend religious services in any given week. This may not seem impressive, but it is a considerably higher percentage than for the countries of Western Europe. Polls in the late 1970s which asked Americans and Europeans about the personal importance of religious beliefs also yield significant results. In the United States 88 percent of those surveyed responded that religious beliefs were "very" or "fairly" important, while the percentages of those in Europe who responded in this same way ranged downwards from Italy's 75 percent to Scandinavia's 45 percent.[5] Such figures should make any observer cautious about dismissing the importance of religion in America, and especially cautious about dismissing the influence of the Christian faith, since it has been the primary religious expression in our history.

Modern polls and the historical record do not, thus, justify the attitude taken by some in our day who paint the history of America with darkest possible colors.[6] If historians of America used to talk of its past as if it revealed the unalloyed progress of freedom, prosperity, and virtue, others today now speak of it as an unalloyed tale of oppression, exploitation, and alienation. Similarly, while many Christians continue to look upon American history as if it were uniquely Christian, some believers have now come to picture that same history as the epitome of sinful arrogance and callousness.

We do not subscribe to either of these extremes. We feel, rather, that America has had a generally religious past. And we feel that its history is liberally sprinkled with genuine Christian influences radiating from lives of exemplary belief.

As much as we acknowledge Christian influences in United States history, however, we still wish to call into question the assumption that just because many Christians have done many Christian deeds in America, the country enjoys simply a "Christian heritage." There are too many problems with this assumption. The chapters which follow offer extended discussion of those problems. Yet it would be appropriate here to state some of them briefly.

CRUCIAL QUESTIONS

One set of questions has to do with how much Christian action is required to make a whole society Christian. Another way of stating the same issue is to pose it negatively—how much evil can a society display before we disqualify it as a Christian society? These kinds of questions are pertinent for all of early American history. When we look at the Puritans of the 1600s, do we emphasize only their sincere desire to establish Christian colonies, and their manifest desire to live by the rule of Scripture? Or do we focus rather on the stealing of Indian lands, and their habit of displacing and murdering these Indians wherever it was convenient? Roger Williams, one of the Puritans himself, asked these very questions and came to much the same conclusion as we have more than 300 years later. Again, do we place more emphasis on the Massachusetts Puritans' desire to worship God freely in the new world or their persecution (and, in four cases, execution) of Quakers who also wished to be free to worship God in Massachusetts?

In the age of the American Revolution the same questions are pertinent. Do we praise American patriots for wanting to be free of Parliament's restraints upon their freedom, or condemn them for taking away freedom of speech and press from their opponents?

Likewise, do we praise American patriots for their defense of "natural law" and "unalienable right," or condemn them for failing to heed Paul's injunctions in Romans 13 to honor their legitimate rulers?

The same questions apply to the period between the Revolution and the Civil War. How do we bring together our assessment of the great evangelistic and reform movements, which did so much to spread biblical righteousness in the country, with inhuman treatment of black slaves and Indian outcasts? Obviously, the need in responding to these sorts of considerations is for a balance that can acknowledge both good and evil in our past and come to conclusions that take both sides into account.

Another problem has to do with Christian use of secular thought. Beginning about the middle of the 1700s, at the time of the French and Indian War, many Americans began to mix their politics and their Christian faith thoroughly and often indiscriminately. Some began to talk about resistance to France, and later to England, as if this were resistance to the Antichrist or Satan himself. During the war against Great Britain, American patriots began to speak about the republican political principles of the Revolution as if these had an almost saving power. Many Christian patriots regarded Americans who were loyal to Great Britain or who wanted to stay out of the conflict as much more than just politically mistaken. They were rather "accursed of God." Then in the early years of the United States, most Christian bodies took the basically secular principles of the American Revolution as the guiding light for organizing churches, interpreting the Bible, and expressing the Christian faith. This process of baptizing political philosophies into the Christian faith was a precarious one. Certainly some of the features of the political philosophy of the American Revolution were commendable from a Christian point of view. But just as certainly they did not deserve to be equated with Christianity or permitted to dictate church structure, interpretations of Scripture, or expressions of the Christian faith. How, then, are we as modern Christians to evaluate our predecessors who seemed to have forgotten that Christianity existed before the creation of American democracy?

A third kind of question involves more theological considerations. Is it, after all, ever proper to speak of a Christian nation after the coming of Christ? From Scripture we know that Old Testament

Israel enjoyed a special status as a nation under God. Modern evangelicals differ among themselves over whether the modern state of Israel remains special as a nation to God. But regardless of how a Christian feels about the modern Jewish nation, is it proper ever to look upon the American nation as the special agent of God in the world? Many great and godly Americans have done so, including Governor John Winthrop in early Massachusetts and President Abraham Lincoln during the Civil War. But were they correct? And what were the practical effects—for the promotion of the gospel or for its harm—when this assumption was made about the Christian uniqueness of America?

These are the kinds of questions which we examine in more detail below. We ask them particularly concerning the early Puritan settlements, the Great Awakening of the colonial period, and the early years of the American nation between the Revolution and the Civil War. But we ask them repeatedly and especially concerning the American Revolution, which is a central theme in almost every chapter which follows. In approaching the Revolution from many different angles, we run the risk of some repetition, a risk which is increased as we pause to draw out the modern implications of ideas and events in the late eighteenth century. But what we hope to gain is a fully satisfactory discussion of the War for Independence and the entire Revolutionary period. For above all else this is the critical event and this is the critical era for the interpretation which regards early America as a distinct source of Christian values, and so they deserve our most careful consideration.

THE PRACTICAL POINT

What is the point, some may ask, in subjecting our ideas about the past to rigorous scrutiny? Even if it turns out that the common picture of an American Christian past is inaccurate, what difference does it make? The difference, we are convinced, is something which profoundly affects the way in which we approach the public arena today. In fact, a true picture of America's past will make Christians today better equipped to speak the gospel in evangelism and to put it to work in social concern.

This book presents in some detail our reasons for questioning whether America has had a predominately Christian past. At the same time, we are convinced that fellow Christians who hold such a view are nevertheless correct in many of their views concerning America's present problems. With them, we deplore abortion-on-demand. We recognize that secular ideas undermine education in public schools. We abhor the ravages of divorce and the weakening of the family. And we feel that American foreign policy should take account of religious persecution in other countries.[7]

We must say also that we share many of the concerns of the smaller number of fellow Christians who have a more negative view of the American past. That is, we also think that American Christians have too often been indifferent to the oppressed and the unrepresented, the very ones to whom the Old Testament prophets, Jesus himself, and the inspired apostles directed our specific attention. We too feel that Americans have trusted far too much in military might and not enough in the strength of the Lord in protecting our property and rights. And we have serious questions about the morality of a defense posture that rests primarily on the threatened use of strategic nuclear arms.[8]

For the purposes of this book, however, we are not concerned if readers share our own views on Christian social policy. Rather, we are concerned to point out how inaccurate views of the past may hamper Christians from mounting the kind of actions that our country and world needs.

Incorrect views of American history are a stumbling block precisely when Christians advance to address public issues. We are hindered in our contemporary Christian efforts if we consider American history as uniformly pernicious. But only a few evangelicals hold this view. So it is not an opinion that we will address at length. The more serious hindrance to positive Christian action in the present is the distorted and overinflated view of America as a distinctively Christian nation. And so we direct most of what follows to redressing the inadequacies of that view.

The final justification for a book like this, if it is written by Christians, must be to clarify our understanding of the gospel and to advance positive Christian action. A view of American history which gives it a falsely Christian character is a hindrance, first, because it distorts the nature of the past. Positive Christian action does not grow out of distortions or half-truths. Such errors lead rather to false militance, to unrealistic standards for American public life today, and to romanticized visions about the heights from which we have fallen.

But a false estimation of America's history also hinders positive Christian action by discouraging a biblical analysis of our position today. And it can compromise genuinely biblical guidelines for action. If we accept traditional American attitudes toward public life as if these were Christian, when in fact they are not, we do the cause of Christ a disservice. Similarly, if we perpetuate the sinful behavior and the moral blind spots of our predecessors, even if these predecessors were Christians, it keeps us from understanding scriptural mandates for action today.

In addition, responsible historical study should also lead to more careful thinking about aspirations for a "biblical politics." The founding fathers in 1776 were much closer to the religious wars of the sixteenth and seventeenth centuries, when nations with competing "biblical politics" fought it out in bloody battle. The founders sought general principles of public life which adherents of all faiths, and none, could accept. There are dangers in their approach, but it also contains strengths which a pell-mell pursuit of a uniquely biblical politics can destroy.

Our historical research has convinced us that two contrasting dangers lurk in wait when we attempt to put the past to use for present purposes. The first danger comes as a result of treating the naturalistic political ideals of American history as if they were on a par with scriptural revelation. This leads to idolatry of our nation and an irresistible temptation to national self-righteousness. The second danger comes from the failure to establish an independent scriptural position over against the prominent values of the culture, a position which allows for selective approval and disapproval of the culture's various values. This failure can lead to secularization, if Christians merely tag along when the culture veers away from God, or it can lead to confusion, when Christians are unable to figure out how public institutions that once supported the faith now work against it. Against both dangers we hope to offer a clearer picture of the past and a more mature understanding of contemporary political concerns.

In the pages which follow, we take pains to point out aspects of Christian faith and practice in early America which we believe are worthy of imitation. But we hope to correct the mistaken assumption that the American past offers an adequate Christian blueprint for our lives today, an adequate biblical standard for responding to public issues, or an adequate understanding of the positive value of pluralistic public policy.

BIBLICAL GUIDELINES

Before we turn in the chapters below to more specific examinations of the various themes and historical matters suggested in this introduction, it would be well to state positively what we consider proper biblical principles for our attitudes to the American nation and its heritage.

In the first place, we must agree with Roger Williams that no nation since the coming of Christ has been uniquely God's chosen people. The New Testament teaches unmistakably that Christ set aside national and ethnic barriers and that he has chosen to fulfill his central purposes in history through the church, which transcends all such boundaries. Samuel Hopkins, a pupil of Jonathan Edwards, reached a similar conclusion at the time of the American Revolution. Hopkins attacked the idea that since God was blessing America in its struggle for independence against Britain, God was somehow designating the nation as his special people and somehow justifying its continuation of slavery. Israel, Hopkins said, could enslave Canaanites because of God's express permission. But this was one of those "many directions and laws to the Jews which had no respect to mankind in general." Now things are different: "the distinction [of Israel] is . . . at an end, and all nations are put upon a level; and Christ . . . has taught us to look on all nations as our neighbors and brethren."[9]

However much particular nations may be used at particular times to do God's work in the world, they are not the primary tools that he is now using. Similarly, the Lord of history has not aligned his purposes with the particular values of any given country or civilization.

Instead, God calls out his people to be strangers and pilgrims, as many of America's early settlers knew. He calls them to repent of their sins and to avoid conformity with the world. We are to be good citizens, but we must remember that our real home, that city with foundations, is beyond our own culture. Our renderings to Caesar, while they must be taken seriously, are to follow the values of that Kingdom which stands above all earthly authority. These priorities, rather than those of our culture and nation, demand our unfettered loyalty.

A second principle is that God has no interest in religion *per se*. There are strong indications, in fact, that he hates religion that is not truly Christian more than the absence of religion. Christ condemned the Pharisees because not only were they blind, but as religious leaders they misled others. "I hate the sound of your solemn assemblies," the prophet Amos informed religious men and women of the Old Testament, when they used their religion as an excuse not to face the Lord himself. One of the biggest dangers of an awareness of America's religious past is the temptation to condone religion *per se* as the means to the ends of national righteousness.

There is the implicit tendency among uncritically patriotic Christians to confirm any religion that tends to uphold the basic principles of American morality. Where is the prophetic voice that condemns all religion which does not have its ultimate end in the God of our Lord Jesus Christ? We must recognize that the American civic faith constantly repeats the chorus that any religion is good enough and that none should claim exclusive truth. Against this tenet, we must be willing to stand as lonely prophets whose hearts are not glad with mere religiosity. Jehovah demands exclusive loyalty.

A third principle is that God judges people not according to what they say they believe but according to their real faith commitment. God always is very practical in this respect. We are liars, he says, if we claim to love God while we are busy hating our brother. Similarly, when Israel would parade her religiosity, God would remind her people of the social injustice that was everywhere practiced upon the powerless. This is the message of the book of James. Real Christian faith can always be evaluated by the fruit it bears. Real Christian faith will produce works, or it is not genuine faith. According to this principle, we should evaluate the righteousness of any society not merely by the religious professions that people make, but also by the extent to which Christian principles concerning personal morality and justice for the oppressed are realized in the society.

The basis for judging the righteousness of this nation at any point is not solely to examine the membership rolls of the churches. No doubt, professions of faith are important. But we must also look at the extent to which believers are engaged in the task of applying Christian love and justice to every facet of life. What is really important is not the claims about an American Christian heritage, nor an unjustifiable equation of modern America with the "my people" of 2 Chronicles 7:14. What will stand in the final analysis is how believers, who recognize that their final Kingdom is not of this world, prove their faith in God by works of worship and love.

A final word is in order about the polemical nature of this book. The views which it presents do, in fact, attempt to rebut some opinions of those who speak much about America's Christian past. Our intent in making this rebuttal, however, is not vindictive. It is meant as a positive contribution to responsible Christian action today. Just as each of us have benefited, either directly or indirectly, from some of those who make such claims about America, so we offer this contribution as a way of helping them to carry on their work for Christ's Kingdom with greater truth and effect.

THE SEARCH FOR CHRISTIAN AMERICA: NOTES

[1]For further details on such Bicentennial activities, see John Woodbridge, Mark Noll, and Nathan Hatch, *The Gospel In America: Themes in the History of America's Evangelicals* (Grand Rapids: Zondervan, 1979), pp. 209-212.

[2]For a reliable survey, see Robert Booth Fowler, *Evangelical Political Thought, 1966-1976* (Grand Rapids: Eerdmans, 1982). Many works illustrating and chronicling these recent events are discussed below in the bibliographical essay, Appendix.

[3]For example, Marsden, *The Evangelical Mind and the New School Presbyterian Experience* (New Haven: Yale University Press, 1970); Marsden, *Fundamentalism and American Culture: The Shaping of Twentieth-Century Evangelicalism, 1870-1925* (New York: Oxford University Press, 1980); Marsden, "Perry Miller's Rehabilitation of the Puritans: A Critique," *Church History*, 39 (May 1970); Marsden, "J. Gresham Machen, History, and Truth," *Westminster Theological Journal*, 42 (Fall 1979); Hatch, *The Sacred Cause of Liberty: Republican Thought and the Millennium in Revolutionary New England* (New Haven: Yale University Press, 1977); Hatch, "The Christian Movement and the Demand for a Theology of the People," *Journal of American History*, 67 (Dec. 1980); Hatch, "Elias Smith and the Rise of Religious Journalism in America," in *Printing and Society in Early America* (Worcester, MA: American Antiquarian Society, 1983); Hatch and Noll, eds., *The Bible in America: Essays in Cultural History* (New York: Oxford University Press, 1982), including Noll, "The Image of the United States as a Biblical Nation, 1776-1865," Hatch, "*Sola Scriptura* and *Novus Ordo Seclorum*," and Marsden, "Everyone One's Own Interpreter? The Bible, Science, and Authority in Mid-Nineteenth-Century America"; Noll, *Christians in the American Revolution* (Grand Rapids: Eerdmans for the Christian University Press, 1977); Noll, "Moses Mather (Old Calvinist) and the Evolution of Edwardseanism,"

Church History, 49 (Sept. 1980); Noll, "The Founding of Princeton Seminary," *Westminster Theological Journal*, 42 (Fall 1979); and Noll, "Scientific History in America: A Centennial Observation from a Christian Point of View," *Fides et Historia*, 14 (Fall-Winter 1981).

[4]For example, Marsden, with Frank Roberts, eds., *A Christian View of History?* (Grand Rapids: Eerdmans, 1975); Marsden, Hatch, and Noll, with John Woodbridge and David Wells, *The Eerdmans Handbook to Christianity in America* (Grand Rapids: Eerdmans, 1983); Hatch and Noll, with John Woodbridge, *The Gospel in America: Themes in the Story of America's Evangelicals* (Grand Rapids: Zondervan, 1979); Marsden, "Evangelicals in Wonderland: The Problem of Nonsense," *Christianity Today*, Oct. 13, 1972; Marsden, "The New Fundamentalism," *Reformed Journal*, Feb. 1982; Hatch, "Purging the Poisoned Well Within," *Christianity Today*, Mar. 2, 1979; Noll, "John Wesley and the Doctrine of Assurance," *Bibliotheca Sacra*, 132 (1975); Noll, "The Earliest Protestants and the Reformation of Education," in *The Basis for a Christian School*, D. B. Cummings, ed. (Phillipsburg, NJ: Presbyterian and Reformed, 1982); and Noll, "One Cup, Many Interpretations," *Eternity*, Oct. 1981.

[5]John M. Benson, "The Polls: A Rebirth of Religion?" *Public Opinion Quarterly*, 45 (1981), 580, 582.

[6]This negative view is discussed at length in Chapter 5 below.

[7]On the other hand, we do disagree on some issues with those who hold these views. We do not feel, for example, that lowest-common-denominator prayers in public schools are useful or Christian, and we doubt the necessity for much of our country's expenditures on the military.

[8]On the other hand, we have some disagreements with those who hold these views as well. For example, we feel that wholesale denunciations of capitalism are often overstated, and that unrealistically optimistic views of foreign powers (e.g., U.S.S.R., China) do not aid internal Christian action.

[9]Samuel Hopkins, *A Dialogue, Concerning the Slavery of the Africans* (Norwich, CT: Judah P. Spooner, 1776), pp. 20, 21.

CHAPTER TWO

America's "Christian" Origins: Puritan New England as a Case Study

One of the opinions most persistently and widely held among American evangelicals is that America had essentially Christian origins from which lamentably it turned in the twentieth century.[1] In whatever form such claims are made regarding the United States, they rest heavily on an appeal to the Puritan heritage as the most influential Reformation tradition shaping American culture. Logically it would be conceivable to argue for a laudable Christian foundation for American culture without appealing to the Puritan tradition. Yet if it were shown that the Puritans who settled America did not establish truly Christian cultural principles that were in some important ways perpetuated, then a strong suspicion might be raised that the entire case for a now-lost Christian America rests on rather nebulous foundations.

"CHRISTIAN" CULTURES

The purpose of this chapter is to examine such general claims concerning an original "Christian" base for American culture by looking specifically at some of the cultural achievements of Puritan New England and the Puritan contributions to later American culture. The thesis is that such claims should be highly qualified in the light of the ambiguous character of much of the Puritan cultural achievement and influence. This thesis in turn is based on a more theoretical argument as to whether there are likely to be found any actual historical examples of truly "Christian" cultures. These conclusions finally, and more incidentally, raise some questions about various programs of present-day Christians for the "Christian transformation of culture."

The case of New England is especially intriguing and important because the Puritan leaders had a relatively free hand in shaping their culture according to clearly articulated rules, which they believed were uniquely and consistently Christian. As such they represent an uncommonly ideal "laboratory" in which to analyze the possibilities and pitfalls of a truly Christian culture. In the southern colonies, by contrast, major institutions such as representative government or Negro slavery evolved under circumstances motivated more by material ambition than specifically Christian ideals. The Puritans, on the other hand, could hardly till a field without writing down a Christian rationale. This explicitness and articulateness gave the Puritans a great advantage as shapers of culture. Much of what they said explicitly, other Protestants of the seventeenth century shared implicitly; but the Puritans' articulations gave the ideas distinct shape, both intellectually and institutionally. At least partially for such reasons Puritan conceptions long remained major influences in America. In the most influential American churches Puritan categories were commonplace until the mid-nineteenth century. Except for a number of remarkable southern politicians, almost every prominent American thinker before World War I was either born in New England or educated there. As late as the early decades of the twentieth century many American literary figures were still wrestling with the vestiges of the Puritan heritage. And even more pervasive than such influences on American ideas was the Puritan impact on American values. While Puritanism could not claim to have single-handedly shaped the American conscience, it certainly helped define its most distinctive traits.

The wider community of scholars has long recognized the broad impact of Puritanism in shaping American culture. Typical of the continuing interest in this theme is Sacvan Bercovitch's book *The Puritan Origins of the American Self*, published in 1975, which has been remarkably popular for an academic volume. Bercovitch focuses his exposition on the Puritans' concept of their own identity. Based on their understanding of typologies in the history of God's people, they viewed New England's corporate mission as recapitulating the mission of the Old Testament nation of Israel. The related conclusion that America was chosen by God and destined to lead mankind has been traced by many historians to American Puritan concerns with the covenant and the Millennium. The continuing

American moral fervor has likewise commonly been traced to Puritan origins. And, growing from this, the connection between the "spirit of capitalism" and the Protestant ethic can readily be illustrated in a New England line of descent from Cotton Mather to Benjamin Franklin. In his notable *Religious History of the American People*, Sydney Ahlstrom emphasizes this formative Puritan culture, or, as he puts it, the "dominance of Puritanism in the American religious heritage":

> . . . the future United States was settled and to a large degree shaped by those who brought with them a very special form of radical Protestantism which combined a strenuous moral precisionism, a deep commitment to evangelical experientialism, and a determination to make the state responsible for the support of these moral and religious ideas. The United States became, therefore, the land *par excellence* of revivalism, moral "legalism" and a "gospel" of work that was undergirded by the so-called Puritan Ethic.[2]

Yet, granting the view of Ahlstrom and other scholars that the Puritan influences on American life were indeed large, the issue remains as to whether the Puritans provided a truly Christian basis for American culture. The question is complicated by the fact that "Christian"—like "Puritan"—has a confusing variety of meanings. First, it can have a weak generic meaning as simply describing some connection with the Judeo-Christian heritage. Almost everything in Western culture from the late Roman Empire until about 1800 was "Christian" in this sense. Yet it is clear that there are many such "Christian cultural developments"—the Thirty Years War and persecution of the Jews and the Waldensians, for instance—of which we would not approve.

A second common use of the term *Christian* and related terms refers to the presence of many individuals in a culture who were apparently Christians. A brief reflection indicates that the presence of Christians is no guarantee that the cultural activities they pursue warrant our approval. Many Christians today, for instance, disapprove of South African racial policies even though these are promoted by apparently sincere Christians. Throughout history many genuine Christians, even when they have been attempting to apply their Christian principles to guide their cultural activities, have turned out to be drastically mistaken.

If we wish to talk about Christian cultural activities in an evalua-
tive way, then, we will have to indicate that we have a third and more
restricted meaning in mind. We will mean cultural phenomena produced by apparently Christian persons who not only are attempting
to follow God's will but who in fact succeed reasonably well in doing
so. That is, although we would not expect perfection, we would
expect that a "Christian" society in this sense would generally distinguish itself from most other societies in the commendability of both
its ideals and its practices. Family, churches, and state would on the
whole be properly formed. Justice and charity would normally be
shown toward minorities and toward the poor and other unfortunate
people. The society would be predominantly peaceful and law-
abiding. Proper moral standards would generally prevail. Cultural
activities such as learning, business, or the subduing of nature would
be pursued basically in accord with God's will. In short, such a
society would be a proper model for us to imitate.

NEW ENGLAND AS A TEST CASE

Was Puritan New England such a model Christian culture? The
Puritans thought of themselves as a "city on a hill" for the world to
imitate. In fact, their culture did display many admirable features.
Yet their achievements were flawed in some basic and most ironic
ways. The corruption of the best often becomes the worst. And in
this case, some of the best of Puritan principles were transformed for
the worse in the actual historical setting. Most ironically, probably
the principal factor turning the Puritan cultural achievement into a
highly ambiguous one was the very concept that is the central theme
of this chapter—the idea that one can create a truly Christian culture.

Viewed from evangelical Protestant perspective, the Puritans indeed seem to have started with many of the best of principles. The
presupposition of Puritan thought was that the Triune God had
revealed himself preeminently in Scripture. Scripture, then, through
God's gracious illuminating work among the regenerate, was the
only sure guide to God's truth. Everything that one did had therefore to be based on biblical principles. Although Scripture might not
reveal everything one needed to know (reason must be a subordinate
guide), Scripture touched on a great deal, and persons were to be

guided by it wherever it spoke. Especially in the area of redemptive concerns, the Bible was a complete guide. Hence with respect to the church one was to do nothing that went beyond Scripture. This initially was the issue that separated Puritans from Anglicans in the late sixteenth century. Both accepted the authority of Scripture; yet Puritans saw the Bible as regulative on every subject on which it spoke, even to the wearing of wigs, for instance. With respect to the conduct of the church, the Puritans' fundamental principle was not only to do what was consistent with Scripture, but to do nothing that was not commanded by Scripture. Certainly the Puritans could not be faulted for neglect of the principle of *sola Scriptura*. Indeed, if they had a fault in this area, it was in sometimes pushing this good principle to an extreme.

Their essential theological principles seem consistent also with much that is laudable in the evangelical heritage. Their theology was essentially in the tradition of Calvin, especially in emphasizing the sovereignty of God, human inadequacy, dependence solely on God's grace, and the necessity of centering all of life toward the end of glorifying God.

With respect to expressions of basic motives, Puritan society accordingly appears especially commendable. Both publicly and privately God's sovereignty and the necessity of dependence on his will were widely recognized.

Furthermore the moral standards to which most of the population apparently subscribed appear to have been extremely high. God's law was intensely studied and in principle respected. Unquestionably the presence of such high ideals had some very positive cultural effects—in family life, respect for neighbors and their rights, concern for the poor, avoidance of ostentation, expressions of reverence for God's name, and the like. The line, of course, between morality arising out of genuine piety and that arising from formal legalism is a thin one, and no doubt the Puritans often transgressed into the latter, as their opponents were fond of pointing out. Nevertheless, one could hardly doubt that the vigorous introduction of biblical moral standards had a generally commendable influence in their cultural life.

Coming Up Short?

On this score, however, the Puritans themselves were the first to emphasize how far short they fell of their own standards. Their own very realistic accounts of the state of their society make clear that if moral practice is to be the gauge for whether a culture is "Christian" in a strict sense, even the Puritans are hardly a reliable model to imitate. All throughout their history in America, Puritan leaders regularly preached "Jeremiads" to their people. These bewailed indifference to God, callousness of social relationships, profanation of God's will, and disregard of holiness. To the preachers of Jeremiads, whose sermons could be heard as soon as the first settlers arrived and as long as the tiniest spark of Puritanism remained in America, the morality of early America was always less than it should have been.

But this was far from the only problem. The Puritan grasp of crucial aspects of the Christian life often came much more from the common assumptions of their age than from eternal principles. Their harsh attitudes toward outsiders—toward Indians, for instance, who were abused as "Canaanites" in America's "Promised Land"—are hardly models that we should imitate.

While it would be impractical here to attempt to weigh the relative success or failure of each aspect of the Puritan experiment, in their central effort in culture building—that of establishing a civil government—we can see most sharply the difficulties of establishing a truly "Christian" society. In founding their government, the Puritans started with the commendable principles just described. John Winthrop, the first governor of Massachusetts Bay, the principal Puritan colony, had formulated a very precise social-political rationale even before his ship touched American shores. Starting with the premise that God's glory should be made manifest in human affairs, Winthrop outlined how those who love God should live. His summary was essentially Augustinian—with a serious view of human moral failure and a high view of God's sovereign grace—and biblical. Those who glorified God should keep his law. With respect to social relationships it is "commanded to love his neighbor as himself; upon this ground stands all the precepts of the morrall lawe, which concerns our dealings with men."[3] Such a conception of the ideal for the relationships and attitudes of Christians seems, at the least, a good start.

A New Israel

The central problem, however, immediately presented itself when

Winthrop, the civil governor, attempted to apply the summary of the law to the entire society of Massachusetts Bay. While he made the distinction between justice, which should be expected in any society, and mercy, to be found in Christian associations, he clearly considered the entire Massachusetts society as such to be essentially Christian. In making this assumption Winthrop was, of course, only reflecting a point generally taken for granted since the latter days of the Roman Empire—that Western society was at least in principle, or at the very least in potential, Christian. Winthrop expressed this assumption in typically Puritan covenantal form, from which the Puritan conception of the American enterprise followed. The Old Testament clearly taught that God dealt with nations according to covenants, either explicit or implicit, the stipulations of which were God's law. Covenant-breaking nations were punished; covenant-keeping nations were blessed. The people of God, Israel in Old Testament times and the church in the New Testament age, stood of course in a special relationship to God. If they were constituted as a political entity, and here Israel seemed obviously the model to imitate, then they should make their social-political covenant explicit, following the examples in the Pentateuch. This is precisely what Winthrop and his fellow Puritans thought they were doing. They were becoming a people of God with a political identity, and so they stood in precisely the same relationship to God as did Old Testament Israel. Bercovitch explains this equation in terms of typology:

> Sacred history did not end, after all, with the Bible; it became the task of typology to define the course of the church ("spiritual Israel") and of the exemplary Christian life. In this view Christ, the "antitype," stood at the center of history, casting His shadow forward to the end of time as well as backward across the Old Testament. Every believer was a *typus* or *figura Christi*, and the church's peregrination, like that of old Israel, was at once recapitulative and adumbrative.[4]

Winthrop assumed that he could transfer the principles of nationhood found in ancient Israel to the Massachusetts Bay Company with no need for explanation. He accordingly based his argument that love summarizes the law of the land directly on the Old Testament covenant. "Thus stands the cause between God and us," he affirmed. "We are entered into Covenant with him for this worke. . . ." If God heard this company's prayers, he went so far as to say, and "bring us in peace to the place wee desire," [that is, if the ships make it safely to Massachusetts] "then hath hee ratified his Covenant and sealed our Commissions [and] will expect a strict performance of the Articles contained in it. . . ." Quoting directly from Moses' farewell in Deuteronomy 30, Winthrop concluded with the promise of either blessings or curses dependent on the observance of the law:

> Beloved there is now sett before us life, and good, deathe and evill in that wee are Commaunded in this day to love the Lord our God, and to love one another to walke in his wayes and to keepe his Commaundements and his Ordinances, and his lawes, and the Articles of our Covenant with him that we may live and be multiplyed . . . or perishe out of the good Land. . . .[5]

Here, before the main body of Puritans ever set foot on American shores, is compressed in Winthrop's thought the paradoxical character of almost the entire Puritan enterprise. They believed their vision for the transformation of human culture was grounded solely on the best principles drawn from Scripture. Yet their historical experience—a tradition of over a thousand years of living in "Christendom," a concept that classical Protestantism did not dispel—led them to interpret Scripture in an ultimately pretentious way that gave their own state and society the exalted status of a New Israel. Some of the results of this identification were laudable, such as the awareness of the need to depend on God in human affairs, the recognition of the fact that states are ordained by God, and a clear affirmation of the rule of law.

But these positive accomplishments were offset by more dubious practical consequences. Old Testament law was directly if not exclusively incorporated into the legal systems of New England. So we find the Massachusetts "Body of Liberties" of 1641 stating that "if any man after legall conviction shall have or worship any other god, but the lord god, he shall be put to death." The same penalty was prescribed, together with the corresponding Old Testament citations, for witchcraft, blasphemy, murder, sodomy, homosexuality, adultery, and kidnapping.[6] Such laws were not all without precedent in English Common Law and elsewhere; yet here the Old Testament texts were copied directly into the New England law books. The most notorious cases of a major miscarriage of justice in New England were the Salem witchcraft executions. Although not as extensive as many similar incidents in Europe, and resulting from a temporary social hysteria, nonetheless they were based legally on the assumption that New England law should duplicate that of ancient Israel.

Although sincere efforts were made to keep church and state technically separate, in fact it was the state that established the church in the colonies, saw to it that only true religion was taught, required church attendance, banished dissenters, and even called church synods. In Massachusetts Bay the voting franchise was limited to church members, with the corollary that only church members were eligible for public office. Behind all the practical confusion of church and state was the overriding presumption that New England was the New Israel.

Nowhere do the dangers of this assumption become more clear than in the Puritans' treatment of the native Americans. Since the Puritans considered themselves God's chosen people, they concluded that they had the right to take the land from the heathen Indians. Again, they had explicitly biblical rationale for their policies. They regarded themselves as the new political Israel; but it was a case of mistaken identity. The result was worse than if they had made no attempt to find a Christian basis for politics. As a book published in 1981 by Henry Warner Bowden, *American Indians and Christian Missions*, shows, even commendable missionary motives could not overcome the profound and inhuman prejudice which the Puritans bore to the native Americans. What this and other studies reveal is how regularly Puritans even used a Christian rationale to justify the exercise of pride and selfish interest at the expense of the Indians.

Roger Williams and a Challenge to the New England Way

The paradoxes in the "Christian" ideals of the main body of New England Puritans become more apparent when we contrast their formulations with those of the one person to challenge their crucial assumption regarding Israel and the church, Roger Williams. Williams too may be counted among those Calvinists who contributed to the American heritage, though among Calvinists themselves he represented a minority position. In his view of the church, Williams in a sense was more puritan than the Puritans. Concerned above all else with preserving the purity of the church, he came to the conclusion that this could be accomplished only by the clear separation of the church from the state and society. Williams differed from the vast majority of Calvinists of his era in holding consistently that the church was an essentially spiritual entity made up of those bound together in pure love to God. This conception altered his view of the proper interpretation of the Old Testament and typology. In the prevailing Puritan view, Christ was the antitype toward whom Old Testament history pointed and the principles of the Old Testament age were recapitulated in the church. Williams, on the other hand, while seeing the Old Testament types fulfilled in Christ, in addition held that the church was the spiritual antitype of Israel, rather than a type exactly equivalent to political Israel. So in reference to Old Testament Israel, Williams writes:

> The *Antitype* to this state I have proved to be the *Christian Church* which consequently hath been and is afflicted with spirituall *plagues, desolations,* and *captivities,* for corrupting of the *Religion* which hath been revealed unto them.[7]

In Williams's view, then, even the church was prone to corruption as Israel had been, and surely the civil government did not stand closer to representing purely God's elect nation than did the church. Hence states, far from being potentially new Israels, were a further corrupting influence and had no business trying to enforce principles of true religion.

Thus perhaps we ought to credit Williams as the best exemplar of the truly positive Puritan influence in American culture. His clear separation of church and state with the consequent toleration of religious dissent recommends him as a most attractive figure. So does his refusal to suppose that Englishmen by virtue of their covenant with God had acquired some special right to take land from the native Americans. Yet it is surely ironic to have to present Williams as the chief evidence for the commendable influences of Puritanism on American culture. First, by almost anyone's standards he was something of an eccentric. Second, by the standards of the vast majority of Puritans and their most direct heirs it was precisely for his stand on the relationship of Christianity to culture that Williams was despised, and that he was banished from Massachusetts.

When we look then at the Puritans' efforts to establish the actual structures of a "Christian" society, our quest for finding laudable Christian origins in the American experience ends by being lost in a maze of paradoxes. The principles with which they start seem good enough, and certainly there were many positive achievements. But every culture in history has some good laws and institutions mixed with some bad ones. Puritan New England does not seem to be unusually distinguished in this respect. Despite their strenuous efforts to apply good principles in building a model Christian society that would be a "Citty upon a Hill"[8] for the world to imitate, we are left uncertain that the city in question is the City of God.

THE LONGER-RANGE IMPACT OF PURITANISM ON AMERICAN CULTURE: AN ASSESSMENT

American Principles of Government

Given such uneven foundations, it is not surprising that America's later and more secularized culture accentuated the Puritans' paradoxical traits. Secularization[9] certainly does not correct the fundamental design. Sometimes it may inadvertently improve it, but such alterations are both accidental and haphazard. The unevenness remains, sometimes more spectacular or even grotesque.

Such conclusions apply to the subject of the long-range Puritan contributions to American principles of government—certainly a focal point for the persistent and popular arguments that America had genuine Christian foundations. The cornerstone in such conceptions is the Puritan emphasis on law. Rousas J. Rushdoony puts it this way:

> But, basic to all colonial thought, was the ancient and Christian sense of the transcendence and majesty of law. According to John Calvin, "the law is a silent magistrate, and a magistrate a speaking law."[10]

Such principles had been explicit in the Puritan view of the covenant in which God's law was ordained above both the government and the people. The execution of Charles I in England in 1649 took for granted the centrality of this higher law. John Locke's formulations in the next generation were clearly a secularization of this fundamental concept. Natural law, ordained by the deity and discoverable by reason, reigned above monarchs. By 1776 such conceptions were so widely held in America that the archpropagandist of the Revolution, Thomas Paine, could claim them as common sense. Echoing the Puritan language, Paine suggested that a

> day be solemnly set apart from proclaiming the charter; let it be brought forth, placed on the divine law, the Word of God; let a crown be placed thereon, by which the world may know, that so far as we approve of monarchy, that in America *the law is king*.[11]

As Paine was well aware, this concept had a strongly Christian and Puritan lineage in America. In the terms we have defined, it would qualify as at least generically Christian, and to the extent that we might approve of the higher law idea we should give the Puritans and their heirs the credit for being among the chief promoters of it. Yet giving Puritans credit for promoting such ideas is not equivalent to establishing that the concepts on which American government were based were essentially "Christian" in any strong, positive sense. Even in the weak generic sense there is some ambiguity in identifying the concept as essentially "Christian." After all, the concept has other roots as well—Greek, Roman, Anglo-Saxon, and (as the case of Paine makes clear) Enlightenment. To recognize only the "Christian" aspect is misleading, even though the Judeo-Christian tradition made an important and probably quite laudable contribution.

The Moral Influence of Puritanism

American political developments taken as a whole may yield many "Christian" and Puritan influences, but they do not lead to the conclusion that there was once a properly Christian America. Yet there is at least one more major area where a case can be made for just such a conclusion. This is the area of general moral influence in helping to create a law-abiding citizenry with a strong conscience. Sydney Ahlstrom goes so far as to suggest that this was the principal contribution of Puritanism to American democracy in that "Puritanism almost created a new kind of 'civic person.' "[12] Although the exact connections are, of course, impossible to document definitively, it does appear that Americans were generally well disposed to obey the civil law, to play by the rules in the democratic process, and to bring their actions and those of others under moral review. These dispositions can be traced, at least in part, to the Puritan emphases on God's law as the fundamental basis of their society. Such emphases for the Puritans involved not only the idea that the government was subject to a higher law, but also that all citizens were obliged to keep God's law. The law, said Scripture, was a schoolmaster preparing persons for regeneration; hence it seemed a valuable service for the state to require the entire citizenry to keep the law. Furthermore, since the terms of the covenant stipulated that the society would be blessed or cursed by God, depending on its obedience to the moral law, every citizen had a strong motive both to keep the law himself and to encourage his neighbors to do the same.

Since God's law was the schoolmaster for New England, and New England to a large extent was the schoolmaster for America, Americans in the Puritan tradition indeed seem to have had an unusually highly developed internalized sense of civic and moral responsibility. This "Puritan" conscience in fact still provides an important aspect of the explanation of the periodic eras of reform that shaped American political and social history. Such reforms seem typically to have had middle-class leadership that could not be explained in terms of self-interest of the class itself. The antislavery movement, for instance, had a strong Yankee leadership which saw the progress of the entire nation as retarded by the sins of its southern members. Similarly, although its expressions were in somewhat more secularized terms, the Progressive movement of the late nineteenth and early twentieth century must be explained at least in part in terms of the bad conscience of the otherwise comfortable middle class.

Such attitudes can be related to a general Puritan attitude toward culture, best summarized by the concept of "calling." As was true of Calvinists generally, Puritans emphasized that one's spiritual responsibilities were not confined to the church or devotional life. Rather, in every aspect of one's activities, even the very mundane, one was called to glorify God. Hence one's responsibilities to society, for example to participate in the political sphere and to see that justice was done, were part of one's spiritual vocation. Similarly one's work, whether pastoring actual sheep or God's people, was a sacred duty. Again, to the extent that these ideals reflected proper motives, we latter-day evangelicals would approve of them as properly Christian.

Christianity or Moralism?

Ironically, however, evangelicals today should probably take less pleasure than most other persons concerning the longer-range impact of such Puritan ideals in shaping American culture. The American sense of moral responsibility frequently appears in a predominantly secularized form. It is often a moral sense detached from the gospel of grace. The irony involved is perhaps clearest with respect to the work ethic. The historical prototype here is Benjamin Franklin. His morality has a Puritan lineage indeed; but its actual expression is a works-righteousness detached from the gracious work of Christ. Franklin worked very hard, and he was very successful, but he did it all for himself. Similarly the moral and reform impulses in American society have in their secularized form the character of a religion of moralism. The nation, it is supposed, will save itself by its own works of righteousness. Such moral fervor often becomes an end in itself. The clearest examples are found in the secularized versions of American Protestantism such as Unitarianism and modernism, in which religion became morality. Puritanism indeed helped foster such traditions, but in their secularized versions the offspring of the Puritan ethic turn out to be at best the works-righteousness of Pelagianism, of self-salvation, or even of simple secular moralism.

The weakness of this moralism, which flows directly out of the Revolutionary period, becomes apparent if we contrast it to the views of Jonathan Edwards, the major eighteenth-century American to resist the trends of the age. Edwards defended a full-fledged Augustinian view, insisting that true virtue arises only from loving the Creator, a love that expands one's horizons to love all created beings. Common grace allows unregenerate people to discover some proper principles of fairness, justice, and order. On many practical points they might come to the same conclusions as the regenerated person, but not for the fully right reasons. Fully genuine virtue differs *qualitatively* from similar phenomena among the unregenerate. That qualitative difference arises because true virtue is an affectionate response to being overwhelmed by the gracious love of the Creator.[13] This distinction holds practical importance for politics. While it allows room for cooperation between Christians and non-Christians in civic enterprises, it makes it impossible to think of these enterprises as truly Christian.

Evangelicalism and the Denial of Puritanism

Yet the defenders of a more positive view of Puritanism's contributions to American morality might point out that many American Christians never did bow the knee to the Baal of modernism, let alone Unitarianism, and that among the many conservative Protestants today a healthy Protestant ethic still survives. Even in the 1980s a full one-third of Americans reputedly claim an experience of being born again. American evangelicalism, at least since about 1870, however, provides only more paradoxes in our search for continuations of a truly positive Puritan influence in American culture. Evangelicals also participated in the process of secularization, and as they did some of the chief casualties were valuable aspects of the Puritan ethical tradition. Much of modern evangelicalism and fundamentalism tended to shift the focus in Christianity from God's sovereignty to the personal human experience. Typically the epitome of Christian experience was described as a special act of consecration in which one gave up oneself (as in "laying all on the altar") and allowed Christ or the Holy Spirit to take over. Those who so consecrated themselves attained what they considered to be a life in which they enjoyed at least consistent victory over sin. The spiritual sensitivities, concern for holiness, and evangelistic zeal associated with this position certainly have often been admirable. Yet such perfectionist tendencies in American evangelicalism often involved the contraction of the areas that sanctification touched. The Christian life came to involve largely "spiritual" activities, especially personal devotions, witnessing about one's own experience, and the avoidance of select symptoms of worldliness. It tended also to be strongly individualistic, with relatively little sense of corporate callings or responsibilities.

A crucial aspect of the Puritan ethic was lost in this typically American evangelical ethic. Essential to the Puritan outlook, and certainly one of the great sources of virtue in their whole way of life, was a sense of the inability (even of the Christian) to serve God perfectly. The Puritan's life was hence characterized by continual self-examination and a strong sense of one's own worthlessness before the holiness of God. Such a sense of one's own limitations served as a continual reminder of the necessity to throw oneself entirely on God's grace. This sense of limitation was an essential aspect of the Puritan ethic and an important counter to pretentious tendencies in those who considered themselves specially chosen by God. This applied even to the Puritan concept of the nation, so that self-confidence was limited by recognition of unworthiness, as manifested in the immense Jeremiad literature lamenting the declines of Puritan societies.

The sense of limitation before God was, however, an aspect of the Puritan ethic that could not easily survive the process of secularization. Rather, as the emphasis in the culture generally shifted from God to humans, the sense of human limitation simply tended to disappear. This move away from the Reformation's view of human nature was extensive by the mid-nineteenth century. Soon it even transformed the ethic of most of Puritanism's evangelical heirs. Although American evangelicals and fundamentalists preserved and proclaimed much of the gospel, they paradoxically acted *against* one of the major positive influences which Puritanism had exerted on the moral ideals of American Christians.

The faith of evangelicals—internal, private, perfectionistic, individualistic—denied the public, social, realistic, and communal aspect of Puritan Christianity. Ironically, by the Puritan standard, American evangelicalism itself contributed to the destruction of positive Christian influences in America, a fact that evangelical spokespersons themselves so much lament.

WHY THERE ARE NO CHRISTIAN CULTURES

What is left, then, of the myth of America's "Christian" origins? On the positive side we find that the Puritans approached the task of building a culture with some truly excellent principles and many apparently good motives. Christianity accordingly appears to have had positive influences on early New England culture. Such a claim, however, is considerably less than saying that the culture was essentially "Christian" in a strict sense or even that it had an essentially "Christian" base.

The reason why the Puritans and all similar groups have failed to establish a "Christian culture" seems clear—although the advocates of "Christian culture" appear to ignore it. At the base of every human culture is a shared set of "religious" values that help hold the society together. These values are not simply those of the official organized religion of the culture (although usually such a religion strongly supports such value systems). They are rather those ideals or things that persons in a culture value most highly, are committed to, and would be willing to die for. Most of the traits of this central "religion" in a culture reflect directly the values that predominate in fallen human nature. So, for instance, one factor that we find holding cultures together everywhere is sinful pride. This pride might be manifested in any one of a number of ways, but among the most common have been tribalism, racism, nationalism, and an inflated loyalty to one's own class or social position. Each is a means of convincing a people that they are inherently superior to other peoples and hence that they can treat others as inferiors, even as subhumans worthy of disdain or abuse. Similarly, every human culture is held together by the simple shared values of selfish interest. Putting oneself and one's group first is, in fact, almost the premise on which human governments are based. Other widely held values found in almost every culture are materialism, lust for power, and love of violence. While cultures may be held together also by other values— such as love or respect for elders, respect for law, love of virtue— most of the widely held values related to human nature turn out to be directly antithetical to Christianity.

What happens, then, when Christianity is introduced into such a culture on a large scale? First of all, if the "Christianization" is more than just a formality, many persons in the civilization may live lives radically transformed by God's grace. If sin is substantially reduced in the lives of such saints who control the government, the society may be transformed into something that is reasonably Christian in the narrowest sense—except for some areas that might be missed due to blind spots, misinformation, or prejudices of the age. However, in no society of any considerable size has the overwhelming majority of citizens ever been radically committed Christians. Furthermore, even the greatest saints fail to overcome fully in this life such sins as ride and self-interest, and often even materialism, lust for power, and the love of violence. So a civilization, even if it contains many true Christians, will retain these nearly universal human traits. The introduction of Christianity will indeed improve the civilization, since many persons and some resulting cultural activities and institutions will be shaped by ideals more or less in conformity with God's will.

Alongside the sinful tendencies at the core of a civilization may be important positive tendencies to which Christianity contributes. Hendrikus Berkhof, for instance, has argued that the coming of Christ introduced into Western culture a new concept of the importance of the suffering and the oppressed. "An ordinary street scene, such as an ambulance stopping all traffic because *one* wounded man must be transported, is the result of the coming of the Kingdom." These and similar observations as to Christianity's impact on culture have considerable credibility. Yet it is important to emphasize, as Berkhof does, that these are at best only harbingers of the Kingdom. "They are the crocuses in the winter of a fallen world."[14]

When Christianity is linked as closely to society as Puritanism was to colonial America, it can transform aspects of culture; yet on any large scale or in the long run such transformation will be severely limited by other forces at the base of a society. The gains, although real, will almost always be ambiguous, since in many cases Christianity will be amalgamated with the various anti-Christian forces that distort the foundations of any society. Such ambiguities become particularly strong if the society comes to regard itself as more or less officially "Christian." In such cases the name of Christianity will be superimposed on a culture that retains some essentially anti-Christian features.

Puritan culture, then, for all its merits, can hardly qualify as a model Christian culture. This by no means is to condemn the Puritans, for in many ways they present an attractive and successful example of applying Christianity to cultural activities. Yet just because of this degree of success, they are an excellent example of the inherent limits in attempting to establish a model Christian culture.

What can we say then about the positive "Christian" influences on culture other than that it does good for individuals? Certainly Christianity brings many broad, obviously good influences, as when family lives are improved, charity is displayed, the poor are cared for, high moral standards are pursued, just laws are enacted, personal worth is properly valued, minorities and outsiders are regarded as persons in God's image—all because of more-or-less proper understandings of God's Word. Yet such influences do not result auto-matically from the presence of apparently sincere Christians in a culture. The equation between the number of Christians in a society and the positive cultural results is never a simple one. Often, in fact, the positive influences seem not to predominate. To resolve these apparent paradoxes it may be helpful to use the image of the salt of the earth. That is, Christianity acts as a retardant against the natural tendencies of cultures built on sinful human nature to fall into decay. Such Christian influences are not always obvious, but they may be crucial.

These observations have important implications not only for as-sessing Christian influences in the past, but for our own cultural task. We may speak, as many Christians do, of that transformation which H. Richard Niebuhr described as "Christ the transformer of culture." But as we do, we must retain a realistic view of the limited and often ambiguous accomplishments of Christians in the past. We should be reminded also that we ourselves do not have the final blueprints for establishing the Kingdom of Heaven on earth. We should recognize that we are no more careful students of God's will than were the Puritans, and we are no more exempt from misreading that will than they were. The relationship between Christianity and culture is always reciprocal. The culture transforms the Christian at the same time the Christian transforms the culture. Hence as we assume our responsibilities for the "transformation of culture," we should do so with an equal appreciation for the view that Niebuhr describes as "Christ and culture in paradox."[15]

Yet the combination of these two views does not reduce the urgen-cy or the necessity of our cultural task. If anything, we should use such obligations to apply our Christianity to all areas of life even more urgently. Yet as we do so, we should recognize that the positive effects of Christianity are basically those of mitigating the fun-damentally distorted character of human cultural life. Although the principles of the Kingdom are anticipated by Christian life in this age, anything even vaguely like the full-orbed reality of the King-dom in the progress of culture must await another age.

AMERICA'S "CHRISTIAN" ORGINS: NOTES

[1]See Chapter 6, "Return to Christian America: A Political Agenda?" for a complete discussion of this modern view.

[2]Sydney E. Ahlstrom, *A Religious History of the American People* (New Haven: Yale University Press, 1972), p. 1090.

[3]"A Modell of Christian Charity," in Edmund S. Morgan, ed., *The Founding of Massachusetts: Historians and Sources* (Indianapolis: Bobbs-Merrill, 1964), p. 191.

[4]Sacvan Bercovitch, *The Puritan Origins of the American Self* (New Haven: Yale University Press, 1975), p. 36.

[5]*Op. cit.*, "Modell of Christian Charity," pp. 202-204.

[6]"A Coppie of the Liberties of the Massachusetts Colonie in New England," in Edmund S. Morgan, ed., *Puritan Political Ideas, 1558-1794* (Indianapolis: Bobbs-Merrill, 1965), pp. 197, 198.

[7]Roger Williams, "The Bloudy Tenent of Persecution," in *op. cit.*, *Puritan Political Ideas*, p. 208.

[8]*Op. cit.*, "Modell of Christian Charity," p. 203.

[9]*Secularization* is an ambiguous term that legitimately might be used in a positive way. Here, however, it is intended to mean one of two things that are essentially negative: (1) a debasing of Christianity by a mixture of it with alien elements so that phenomena or ideals that are essentially un-Christian come to be regarded as part of Christianity; or (2) a replacement of Christianity by a new "secular religion," such as Marxism, nationalism, materialism, rationalism, existentialism, individualism, political liberalism or conservatism, etc.

[10]Rousas J. Rushdoony, *This Independent Republic* (Nutley, NJ: Craig Press, 1964), p. 32.

[11]Thomas Paine, "Common Sense," in Loren Baritz, ed., *Sources of the American Mind* (New York: Wiley, 1966), I, p. 145. See also the further discussion of Paine's use of this conception in Chapter 6.

[12]Sydney Ahlstrom, "Thomas Hooker—Puritanism and Democratic Citizenship: A Preliminary Inquiry into some Relationships of Religion and American Civic Responsibility," *Church History*, 32 (Dec. 1963), 423. See also the excellent discussion concerning general Puritan influences in the Revolutionary period by Edmund S. Morgan, "The Puritan Ethic and the American Revolution," *William and Mary Quarterly*, 3rd ser., 24 (Jan. 1967), 3-43.

[13]Edwards's view and the contrast to the prevailing eighteenth-century view of the autonomy of moral philosophy is best described in Norman Fiering, *Jonathan Edwards's Moral Thought and Its British Context* (Chapel Hill: University of North Carolina Press, 1981).

[14]Hendrikus Berkhof, *Christ the Meaning of History* (Richmond, VA: John Knox, 1966), pp. 88, 181.

[15]Richard Niebuhr, *Christ and Culture* (New York: Harper & Row, 1951), pp. 149-222.

CHAPTER THREE

The Great Awakening and the American Revolution

The two most significant events in America during the 1700s were the Great Awakening and the Revolution. The first was a broad revival of Christianity that swept through different parts of the colonies from the late 1720s to the early 1750s, with its most visible manifestations in the early 1740s. The second involved a War for Independence in the 1770s and the creation of a vast new nation, the United States, after Americans defeated the world's greatest military power of the day.

It is not surprising that connections existed between events of this magnitude. One of the most intriguing incidents in the early years of the Revolution, for instance, took place at the tomb of George Whitefield near Newburyport, Massachusetts, in 1775. Whitefield, a tireless traveling evangelist, had been the most visible figure of the Great Awakening. An Englishman, he had crossed the Atlantic thirteen times in the course of a thirty-three-year career in which he preached, on the average, eight or nine times a week (a total of over 15,000 occasions). Exhausted by his constant labors, he had died while on yet another revival tour in America on October 15, 1770.

Now just five years later troops from Massachusetts, Connecticut, and Rhode Island were gathering at Newburyport for a military expedition. Their leader was Benedict Arnold, still a respected general in this time before his defection. Their aim was to capture Quebec and to gain Canadian support in the battle against Britain. Before the expedition set out, however, their young chaplain, Samuel Spring, preached a rousing sermon to the troops. Then he went with some of the officers to Whitefield's tomb. Together they pried off the lid of his coffin, removed the clerical collar and wrist bands from the skeleton, cut them up, and distributed them to the officers.[1] Thirty years before, Whitefield had blessed an American-British force going off to do battle against the French in Nova Scotia. Now the remains of the revivalist were called upon to bless another force, which this time was fighting against the British. (Unfortunately for the Americans, Whitefield's talismans did not work. Arnold and his army were defeated; Canada remained loyal to Britain.)

THE CASE FOR A CONNECTION

It is, however, not just scattered incidents which link the Great Awakening and the American Revolution. Many scholars, secular and Christian alike, have seen more substantial connections. The most influential of these students is Alan Heimert, professor of American Literature at Harvard, who published a painstakingly researched volume in 1966 entitled *Religion and the American Mind from the Great Awakening to the Revolution*. Its argument was that the spirit of the Awakening had become, after the passage of a generation, the vital force behind the Revolution. According to Heimert, the revivalistic Calvinism of the 1740s gradually expanded to become the democratic republicanism of the 1770s. Opponents of the Great Awakening in the 1740s may also have supported the break with England in the 1770s, but only the advocates of the earlier revival grasped the opportunity presented by the later war to forge a democratic America.[2]

Christians who study the American past have sometimes been quick to exploit the work of Heimert and others who echo his conclusions. Their argument takes this form:

1) During the Great Awakening, the population of the colonies was evangelized to an unusual degree.

2) The Awakening raised important Christian themes to new prominence—it called for liberty in Christ; it demanded freedom to worship God; it spotlighted the dangers of spiritual tyranny.

3) These very themes undergirded the struggle for American independence from Great Britain. Or as one student put it, "What was awakened in 1740 was the spirit of American independence."[3]

4) Finally, the implication is sometimes drawn that if the American Revolution was in fact grounded in the Great Awakening, then the Revolution must be considered as much a work of God as the revival itself. This conclusion has appeared frequently since the

celebration of the Bicentennial drew the attention of Christians to the founding events of the country. A forceful statement from 1976 summarized this line of reasoning: "As [colonists] turned from material concerns and humbly sought God in prayer, He healed them and He used it all to bring about the formation of a mighty nation; the United States of America. God then used their repentance to more fully prepare His people for the coming trial of the American Revolutionary War, in which men whom God had chastened and trained were to play major roles. When Colonel Ethan Allen took Fort Ticonderoga, for example, he took it, in his words, 'in the name of the Great Jehovah and the Continental Congress.' "[4]

Is it justified to look at the Great Awakening and the American Revolution in this way? Or to make the question more specific: Does such a view represent good history? And does it represent clear Christian thinking? The facts which speak to both of these more particular questions present a more complicated picture. Yes, definite connections do exist between the Awakening and the Revolution. But, no, these connections provide neither a sufficient explanation for the Revolution, nor a satisfactory Christian evaluation of it. In order to justify these contentions, it is necessary to fill in some background.

THE GREAT AWAKENING

The colonial revival was called a *great* awakening because it touched so many regions and so many aspects of colonial life.[5] In New England the revival energized many of the Congregational churches and inspired the smaller number of Baptists. In the middle colonies the Presbyterians and the Dutch Reformed both benefited from the outburst of concern for personal salvation and daily Christian living. And in the southern colonies, which were affected mostly in the last phases of the Awakening, the revival marked the start of significant growth for Baptists and began to prepare the way for the great Methodist movement of the post-Revolutionary period.

The greatness of the Awakening may also be measured by its most important leaders. George Whitefield was a minister in the Church of England and a friend of John and Charles Wesley.[6] In England he pioneered with preaching in the fields to those whom the churches had passed by. In America, he spoke wherever he could find a pulpit. And he spoke with great power. His message was a simple, Calvinistic one: people needed to recognize their own sinfulness; they needed to turn to God in repentance and faith in order to experience the grace of Christ. Whitefield's ability to move his hearers was legendary. Grown women, so it was said, could be brought to tears when Whitefield pronounced even the single word "Mesopotamia." Benjamin Franklin once calculated that Whitefield could make his voice heard, outdoors, to as many as 30,000 people at one time. Crowds of 10,000 and more were not unusual to hear Whitefield, particularly in the early 1740s when his reputation was at its height.

If Whitefield was the most important preacher of the Great Awakening, Jonathan Edwards was its most important theologian.[7] Edwards himself could be a powerful preacher, as his famous sermon, *Sinners in the Hands of an Angry God,* shows clearly. But he devoted his efforts more to thorough, biblical reflection than to spectacular, public preaching. When critics of the revival condemned it for releasing unregulated emotions, Edwards wrote a careful *Treatise on Religious Affections* to discriminate between true and false religious feeling. Real godliness, he concluded, was demonstrated not by the quantity of emotional release, but by a steady and firm love to God and by a life devoted to following God's law. Edwards later went on to write profound theological works on the human will, on original sin, and on the nature of true virtue. Each of these was a striking example of biblical thinking about God, the human condition, and the way in which God makes his will known to persons. There has never been in America an evangelical theologian as powerful as Edwards, and there have only been a tiny handful of revivalists who can be classed with Whitefield.

The revival they encouraged was a Great *Awakening* because it led, at least for a time, to more dedicated spiritual living. One of the first results of the Awakening was a rapid increase in the number of people making personal profession of faith in order to join a church. In New England, where church records are best, the average number of new members (upon profession of faith) in the Congregational churches of Connecticut was eight per year from 1730 to 1740. But in 1741 and 1742, at the height of the Awakening, the average was thirty-three per year.[8] Comparable rates of church growth were found elsewhere, especially as a result of the work of Baptist revivalists in the Carolinas during the early 1750s.

But other results also testified to the "greatness" of the revival. Jonathan Edwards reported much more intense concern for practical piety in his native Northampton after a series of revivals in 1735 and 1740. In his town, and many other communities, it became customary for individuals to gather for prayer, Bible reading, and personal exhortation during the week. Also as a result of the Awakening, the gospel message came more directly to the downtrodden and the despised. Readers today still find inspiration in the diary of David Brainerd, which Jonathan Edwards edited for publication. And Brainerd was just one of a considerable number of believers whose experiences in the revival led them to devote their lives to mission work among the Indians. The Awakening also stimulated evangelism among slaves, a work in which the Presbyterian Samuel Davies took an especially important part in Virginia. And the Awakening also led to a greater interest in education, both to prepare ministers to spread the gospel and to train laymen in a Christian setting. Although ties with the Awakening were sometimes indirect, several important colleges were founded as a result of its general inspiration—Princeton by Presbyterians in 1746, Brown by Baptists in 1760, Queens (later Rutgers) by Dutch Reformed in 1764, and Dartmouth by Congregationalists in 1769.

In sum, the Awakening had a great impact on individuals, bringing many new Christians into the fold. It had a great impact on the churches, reviving many of them for more active evangelism and daily Christian living. And it had a great impact on colonial culture as a whole, providing new models of public speaking, new motives for public action, and new concern for public responsibility.

THE AWAKENING AND THE CONVERSION
OF THE POPULATION

But did the Awakening shape the Revolution? Is the tie between revived America of 1740 and revolutionary America of 1776 strong enough to say that the good results of the first led to good results in the second? Or is it possible that some of the strength of the colonial revival was drained away by alien forces at the time of the Revolution?

The first question to address is the matter of numbers. Many Congregational churches in New England, many Presbyterian congregations in New York, New Jersey, and Pennsylvania, and many Baptist bodies in the Carolinas took in large numbers of new members when the waves of revival passed by. A longer view, however, shows that the Awakening did not lead to permanent gains in the number of people either attending church or formally becoming members (which usually required a personal profession of faith). In New England, where again records are best, the story is not as encouraging as the large ingatherings for 1741 and 1742 would suggest. In the last years of the decade 1740-1750, the number of those joining churches by personal profession of faith actually declined to levels below those of the 1730s. The result was that the number of people making profession of faith and joining churches for the entire period 1730-1750 amounted to just about the same rate for the entire population as had been witnessed for the thirty or so years before 1730.[9] And in the colonies as a whole, the situation seems to be not even that favorable.

Historians have known for a long time that the number of people in full church membership was surprisingly small in the colonial period. Church members never amounted to more than a third of the population of New England adults, and may never have been as high as 5 percent of adults in the southern colonies. More recently, however, scholars have begun to focus on church "adherence" rather than on church "membership"—in other words, on how many people were associated with churches, and regularly attending, even if they did not formally join.[10] They have found these figures much higher than for comparative figures indicating full church membership. But even these studies of church adherence do not show a significant reversal as a result of the Great Awakening. In fact, the general trend throughout colonial America was toward lower and lower numbers of people "adhering" to churches. The figures, by modern standards (when something like 60 percent of the population belong to churches, but only 40 percent actually attend church regularly), are impressive. But they still show consistent decline. Perhaps as many as 80 percent of the colonial population was regularly connected to churches in 1700, but in a steady decline this figure was reduced to about 60 percent by 1780.[11] The Great Awakening does not seem to have significantly changed this gradual decline. It is therefore not in keeping with the best information now available to say that the Awakening made a significant difference in converting the American population to Christian faith.

THE AWAKENING'S INFLUENCE ON AMERICAN VALUES

There are other ways than mere numbers, however, to see the importance of the Awakening. The revival was, for instance, America's first truly national event. Whitefield and his exploits were common matters for discussion from Maine to Georgia. Ministers from the various colonies corresponded with each other to encourage revival or, in some cases, to caution against its excesses. The Awakening itself also served as a melting pot for the American population. The career of Gilbert Tennent, a Presbyterian evangelist from New Jersey, provides an example of how the revival began to join different groups together. Tennent was born in Ireland of Scottish descent, he attended a small school conducted by his own father in upstate New York, his Presbyterian congregation in New Jersey included some settlers from New England, and at the height of the revival Tennent himself preached as far away from home as Piscataqua, Maine, and Hanover County, Virginia. The revival in short began to provide a set of common experiences for the colonies which marked them off as, together, a unified region distinct from Europe.

In addition, as Americans began to regard themselves more distinctly in colonywide terms, they naturally became more suspicious of churches which retained secure ties with Europe. The most important of these was the Church of England, which was already suspect by some for its close ties with crown officials. After the Awakening, it became a focus of even more suspicion because of its relative indifference to the spread of revival. Such religious feelings had definite political ramifications when tempers between the colonists and the British government began to flare. Suspicion of the Church of England was one more reason for distrusting the British in general.[12]

The Great Awakening also made it respectable to use terms like "liberty," "virtue" and "tyranny" in public discussion. At the time of the revival, to be sure, these terms carried explicitly religious meanings, as Whitefield and like-minded preachers drove home the claims of the gospel. But the very presence of these terms, and the fact that they were great motivators for action, left a permanent legacy. It was far easier, when the tyrant on the horizon was Parliament rather than sin, to make fruitful use of the capital which these terms had acquired in the revival.

The most important effect of the revival on the Revolutionary period, however, was the new model of leadership which it created.[13] The revival was nurtured by traveling evangelists; they called for direct and responsible response from the people; they encouraged lay people to perform Christian services for themselves that were the traditional preserve of the clergy. Whitefield did not read his sermons like so many ministers did in the early eighteenth century. Rather, he used spontaneous extemporaneous forms of address. His speaking style drove home the implicit point that it was not formal education or a prestigious place in the community that mattered ultimately. It was rather the choice of the individual, the common person, for or against God. Whitefield seems to have had almost no thought for politics. But his form of public speaking, and the implicit message of his ministry concerning leadership, constituted a powerful stimulus to a more democratic life. It was not Whitefield alone, of course, who was responsible. But he was the most visible symbol of a vital change in ideas about social hierarchy. His ministry represented the sharpest demonstration of a new confidence in the religious powers of the people. Whitefield was a Calvinist who did not believe in natural human capacity to choose God. But he did believe that God's grace made it possible for even the humblest individual to take a place alongside the greatest of the saints. This spirit—a frank expression of popular democracy and the sharpest attack yet on inherited privilege in colonial America—probably had much to do with the rise of a similar spirit in politics later on.

EVALUATING THE CONNECTIONS

To this point, it is evident that links existed between the colonial Great Awakening and the American Revolution. But it is not clear yet what modern Christians should make of those links. We must push further to see what else we can say about the connection. Our examination of the past must show the same wisdom we would use to examine intriguing questions of our own time. It would be an interesting observation today to note that someone selling a commercial product used a speaking style modeled on the effective evangelistic techniques of Billy Graham. But we would have to go further in examining the situation to see if Billy Graham's specifically Christian concerns were carried over into the sales pitch before we could conclude that the product was a Christian one. That is precisely the place in which we find ourselves now in evaluating the link between the Awakening and the Revolution.

Two kinds of answers may be given to the inquiry which asks if the spirit of the revival led to the spirit of the American Revolution. On one level, it does not seem that this is the case. On another level, it seems to have happened, but with unfortunate results for the Christian message itself.[14]

EDWARDS'S CLOSEST FOLLOWERS AND THE REVOLUTION

In the first instance, it is possible to observe what the closest followers of Jonathan Edwards, the most influential spokesman for the revival, actually did during the Revolutionary period. This would provide clear evidence concerning how those who understood the revival best reacted to the War. Edwards died in 1758, but many of those who studied with him, or who avidly read his books, lived throughout the Revolutionary period, and in some cases even into the next century.

The record here is quite clear. During the Revolution the closest followers of Jonathan Edwards were either strangely indifferent to the struggle for independence, or they were patriots who yet on the basis of their Christian beliefs criticized different aspects of the Revolution. Joseph Bellamy, who studied personally with Edwards, and who was one of his two closest friends, illustrates the indifference.[15] Bellamy was a minister in Litchfield County, Connecticut, for over fifty years (1739-1790). During the War, he did help those in his region who went to fight against the British, and he was generally sympathetic with the cause. But Bellamy also continued to insist that the most important thing, regardless of how the course of political events went, was freedom found in Christ. He once expressed this sentiment directly to his son in early April 1775, just a fortnight before the actual fighting with Great Britain began at Lexington and Concord: "My desire and prayer to God is, that my son Jonathan may be saved. And then, whatever happens to America or to you, this year or next, you will be happy forever."[16] Bellamy was a patriot, but for him the same eternal values that had been most important for Whitefield and Edwards remained, even during the crises of the Revolution, his highest value.

Other close followers of Edwards were more energetic in support of the Revolution, but they too expressed their revivalistic convictions in ways that were unusual for the times. Samuel Hopkins was, after Bellamy, Edwards's closest professional friend.[17] By the time of the War, Hopkins had become pastor of a Congregational church in Newport, Rhode Island, where he expressed both support for independence and criticism for American life. Hopkins was a patriot. Even more he was a child of the colonial Great Awakening. He was, therefore, able to separate his politics from his Christianity enough to criticize American society out of his explicit Christian convictions.

Specifically, Hopkins was troubled about the practice of Negro slavery in America. In a pamphlet published in 1776 and sent to the members of the Continental Congress, Hopkins asked pointedly how the colonies could complain about "enslavement" from Parliament when they practiced a much worse slavery themselves. Hopkins wondered what slaves must think about the colonists' claims against Great Britain when "[Negroes] see the slavery the *Americans* dread as worse than death, is lighter than a feather, compared to their heavy doom; and [this so-called enslavement by Parliament] can be called liberty and happiness, when contrasted with the most abject slavery and unutterable wretchedness to which they are subjected." Hopkins, further, called upon his readers to "behold the *sons of liberty*, oppressing and tyrannizing over many thousands of poor blacks, who have as good a claim to liberty as themselves."[18] The practice of slavery was grossly inconsistent with the patriots' rhetoric. Were not slaves also people made in the image of God? Did not the slave trade wantonly violate the sixth commandment against murdering and the eighth against stealing (i.e., by kidnapping Africans)? And most importantly, did not the practice of slavery by supposedly Christian people hamstring the proclamation of the gospel?

Such questions were heard only rarely in the colonies during the Revolution where British evil loomed as the major menace. It was not mere happenstance that they came from a New Light (i.e., a follower of the revival). The Great Awakening had shown Hopkins what was most important in life. Hopkins's commitment to Christianity was stronger than his commitment to the American colonies. As such, and because of the carefully constructed theological ethics he inherited from Edwards, Hopkins did not let Revolutionary patriotism overwhelm his Christian beliefs. Because he continued to follow the New Light with unswerving vision, he was able—even in the crucible of the Revolutionary trauma—to put first the Kingdom of God.

This kind of criticism of America from patriotic Christians was unusual during the War. But it came also from others who were self-consciously trying to carry on the Awakening's emphases concerning conversion and the Christian life. Other followers of Edwards, like Jacob Green in New Jersey or Levi Hart in Connecticut, also called the new American government to task for continuing to allow slavery at the very time it complained of a "slavery" from Parliament.[19]

The leader of the Baptists in New England, Isaac Backus, made a similar complaint.[20] Except for the question of baptism, Backus remained firmly committed to the teaching of the Great Awakening, even to the extent of referring to the great theologian of the revival as "our Edwards." If colonists were fighting England for liberty, Backus asked, why do the colonies themselves not grant liberty to their own residents? Backus had been forced to witness his fellow Baptists suffer indignities, and sometimes the loss of property or personal freedom, at the hands of the Congregational church-state establishments in Massachusetts and Connecticut. Although Backus supported the drive for independence once the War began, he had been ambiguous earlier. As late as 1771 New England Baptists had appealed directly to King George III, whom other colonists would vilify in the Declaration of Independence five years later. Their complaint was that Massachusetts was treating its "dissenters" (the Baptists and other similar groups) just as poorly as Parliament was treating colonial political dissent. Backus had learned from the Great Awakening that the church must be free to govern itself, as a natural consequence of the liberty of the gospel. He did not see the American colonies encouraging that kind of freedom, even as they took up arms against Britain, and so he expressed his disapproval.

What conclusion may we draw from close followers of Edwards who were either indifferent to the War for Independence, or who treated it as a secondary matter compared to specifically Christian concerns? We are forced to conclude that whatever kinds of connections existed between the revival and the Revolution, it is not appropriate to consider them as two expressions of the same spirit. Sons of the revival supported the Revolution, but they supported even more the truths of the gospel and their practical applications. And these matters, which were of ultimate concern, did not always coincide with the struggle for a new United States. The Great Awakening, therefore, had a more distinctly spiritual character, and it called people to more directly biblical practice than did the Revolution. If the most direct heirs of Edwards saw this, we should too.

HARMFUL CONNECTIONS

On another level, however, it is possible to see closer ties between the Awakening and the Revolution. But these ties should prove disconcerting to modern Christians. Again, to see the nature of these connections, some background is necessary.

The Great Awakening had cut through colonial society like a two-edged sword. The havoc it wreaked was particularly great in New England where personal, ecclesiastical, and social concerns had long been joined together in a distinctive Puritan synthesis. Originally this synthesis had been founded on the regeneration of the individual heart and the subsequent effort to purify church and society for the service of Christ. By the early eighteenth century, however, the stress had come to rest more and more on the sanctifying character of a covenanted society and less and less on the personal covenant of grace underlying the scheme.[21]

The Great Awakening attacked this synthesis mercilessly. First, the theological parties it spawned made a mockery of the ideal of a unified Christian society.[22] Some followers of the revival—the Separates or radical New Lights—went so far as to form entirely new churches, free, as they saw it, from the encrusted decadence of the New England Way. Other, more moderate New Lights, like Edwards himself, worked within the system for a purification of the established churches. A third group, the Old Calvinists, appreciated the gospel message of the Awakeners but feared greatly that the stirrings of revival would destroy the Christian society that had been so lovingly maintained in New England. A final group, the Old Lights, had nothing good to say of the revival whatsoever. To these forerunners of Unitarianism the revival was foolishly archaic in doctrine and destructively enthusiastic in practice. Where New England had presented something of a united front before the Awakening, it was rent afterwards into at least four distinct, mutually antagonistic parties.

An even more fundamental division also arose when the Awakening called the whole Puritan enterprise into question. The Awakeners, or New Lights, urged *individuals* to turn in repentance and faith to Christ. They urged those who heeded their message to purify the churches of all who were not converted. The opponents of the revival, or Old Lights, feared for the safety of New England *society*. They wanted the churches kept open to society at large as a means to sanctify the whole culture.

After the Great Awakening, it was impossible any longer to think of society as the Puritans had done. Those who opposed the revival took over the Puritan conception of a unified society, but greatly deemphasized the need for personal faith to ground the society. On the other hand, those who promoted the revival retained the Puritan conviction about the need for personal salvation, but largely abandoned the Puritan concern for a united commonwealth. The Great Awakening forced a choice. The result was the end of Puritan ideas about society, state, and politics.

The demise of a Puritan conception of society was not in itself necessarily evil. For over 200 years American evangelicals have conceded that Puritans had joined church and state together in harmful ways. In Puritanism there was too much potential for the concerns of the state to overwhelm the demands of the gospel. There was always the chance that the larger concerns of society would overthrow the specific needs of the church. The problem, then, is not so much that the Puritan conception of society was abandoned after the revival.

The problem was rather that leaders of the Awakening did not propose an alternative to the Puritan theology of society. They were so engrossed in valuable evangelistic tasks, and so concerned about nurturing spiritual life in the congregations, that they offered no alternative to the Puritan sociology. They suggested no biblically rooted framework for politics and society to take the place of the Puritan ideas they had rejected. In particular they closed their eyes to the growing diversity within America and for the need to find biblical principles for working in a political situation where no one Christian group would be in control. They seemed to think that if they could only be successful at evangelism, the problems of politics would take care of themselves. But they didn't.

MISPLACED MILLENNIALISM

The lack of an Awakening politics was only part of the problem, however. The Awakening had also raised expectation that the millennial Kingdom of Christ was about to dawn. Edwards himself in the early days of the revival speculated aloud whether the coming Kingdom might not begin with the evangelistic successes in New England. Later, as revival fires cooled and life returned to conditions that had prevailed before 1740, Edwards turned from this idea and saw hope for the future only in the activity of God's people wherever they might be. He, for one, soured on the idea that America would become the New Jerusalem. But others hung on to the millennial vision and continued to speak about events in America as if they were directly related to God's plan for the End of the Age.

These millennial convictions about America, combined with the absence of a Christian theory of politics to replace the discarded Puritan vision, resulted in utter disaster. Christians who had discarded the Puritan conception of an organic Christian society, but who had not formulated a newer biblical conception, were swept off their feet by the powerful patriotic emotions of the Revolution. Proponents of the Awakening, who had grown accustomed to reading the signs of the times in connection with the revival, now thought they could do it in the political sphere as well.

The nature of this disaster, and its connections with the Great Awakening, can be seen most clearly in what happened to the millennial expectations. Particularly when the revival fires seemed to fade in the 1750s, New Lights wondered whether their eschatological hopes had been justified. At this crucial juncture, the French and Indian War offered to many a way to revive the flagging millennial dream. Might not the defeat of popish, tyrannical France be the next step in the coming of the Kingdom? Might not it now be time to translate the spiritual vision of Jonathan Edwards into something much more substantial? Recent scholarship has shown conclusively that this was indeed the tack taken by some New Lights in the 1750s.[23] In 1756, for example, the revivalist Presbyterian from Virginia, Samuel Davies, spoke of the conflict between the Protestant British empire and the Catholic French empire as "the commencement of this grand decisive conflict between the Lamb and the beast." The defeat of the French, Davies held, would produce nothing less than "a new heaven and a new earth."[24]

Changes of opinion about the Last Days which took place during the French and Indian War also determined responses to the Revolution. Of course, one significant alteration had to be made in the millennial vision. As struggle with Britain grew more intense after the end of the French and Indian War in 1763, sons of revival concluded that they had made a mistake in their analysis of that war. These colonists came to think that it was not so much Roman Catholic, French tyranny that was the Antichrist as it was tyranny itself! And who was the embodiment of tyranny in the late 1760s and the early 1770s but Parliament, George III, and the entire British assault on American liberty? The abuse which such thinking led to is illustrated by a sermon on Revelation 13 preached by Samuel Sherwood of Weston, Connecticut in 1776. Sherwood held that British oppression of the colonies was the work of the Antichrist. The seven-headed beast that John described in Revelation 13 was nothing else, Sherwood said, than "the corrupt system of tyranny and oppression, that has been fabricated and adopted by the ministry and parliament of Great Britain."[25]

The millennialism which Edwards and his closest followers had come to see in spiritual terms became for others by the time of the Revolution a religiously sanctioned political device. Because America seemed about to receive the millennial Kingdom on its shores, the struggle against Parliament could be translated into a holy war for God against the Antichrist.

CONFUSING CHRISTIAN AND POLITICAL LOYALTIES

The debasement of eschatology was, unfortunately, not the only problem. In the absence of a well-articulated, biblical framework for thinking about society, American Christian leaders had no means to make critical discrimination about the ideology of the Revolution itself.[26] That ideology is discussed more directly in the next chapter, but for now the question is not whether Revolutionary thought was compatible with the Christian's faith. The important thing is rather to see the confusion which took place between biblical, Christian categories and categories of political philosophy and patriotic nationalism. This happened in at least three ways. In the first, Christian leaders spoke as if it were more important for fellow believers to make the proper choice against Britain than it was to maintain spiritual unity around the gospel.

In 1775 a group of Presbyterians from Philadelphia, where the Continental Congress was in session, urged fellow Presbyterians in North Carolina to support the Congress and their local patriot associations. If the Carolinians could not do so, the Philadelphia Presbyterians wrote, "you will effectually prevent our missionaries from visiting you, as ministers of the gospel of peace." And they went on to further warnings if their fellow Presbyterians would not enlist in the patriotic cause: "If you now desert the cause of liberty; if you suffer yourselves and your children, and children's children, to be stript of all the well earned fruits of honest industry, at the will of a [Parliamentary] Minister or his placemen and friends; if you will offer yourselves to voluntary slavery, and desert the loyal sons of liberty of all denominations in the most honourable and important context, we can have no fellowship with you; our soul shall weep for you in secret, but will not be able any longer to number you among our friends, nor the friends of liberty."[27] Be their theology or Christian life what it may, if Carolina Presbyterians would not support the Revolution, they were not worthy of the Christian fellowship of their brothers in Philadelphia.

In the second place, it became common for believers during the Revolution simply to equate loyalty to the new nation and loyalty to Christ. Moses Mather of Connecticut condemned Thomas Hutchinson, the last British governor of Massachusetts, for his support of the crown. And Mather boldly proclaimed that for his "crimes" against America, Governor Hutchinson would suffer a "condign punishment hereafter."[28] Nathaniel Whitaker of Salem, Massachusetts, pronounced the "curse of Meroz" (from Judges 5:23) on those loyal to the crown and said that they were "accursed of God."[29] And

Robert Smith of Pequa, Pennsylvania, said it most directly: "The cause of America is the cause of Christ."[30]

In the third instance, patriots tied their own politics so closely to Christian virtue that they lost the capacity to be self-critical, the very capacity which the closest followers of Edwards retained throughout the period. The most striking example of this failure probably took place early in the War. The Rev. Alexander MacWhorter of Newark, New Jersey, was serving as a chaplain with Washington's troops in the dark days toward the end of 1776. The American forces were being pressed hard by the British as they straggled across New Jersey from New York to Philadelphia. On December 7, MacWhorter preached a memorable sermon of condemnation against the Scottish troops who made up part of the pursuing British army. MacWhorter called them "Papist Highland barbarians," even though most of them were really Presbyterians like himself. It was a sermon which deeply moved the thousands of bedraggled troops who heard it. But the irony was that, full of condemnation for British evil as the sermon was, MacWhorter never said one word about the 200 or more camp-following women, perhaps the largest gathering of prostitutes to that day on American soil, who with the troops listened to his sermon.[31]

CONCLUDING OBSERVATIONS

American Christians in the late twentieth century should be appalled at the way in which the Bible, and Christian categories generally, were abused in these several ways in the Revolution.[32] During the emotional fervor of the War patriots invested their cause with the kind of honor that belonged to God alone. It is simply not possible to see how such travesties could have gone on, had not American believers neglected to construct biblical approaches to society and politics after the collapse of Puritan convictions as a result of the Great Awakening. We cannot blame Edwards and Whitefield for the way in which their spiritual descendants abused the Bible and confused allegiance to God and allegiance to patriotism during the Revolutionary War. We can blame their followers, and even those believers who differed with them, for not building a new theology for applying Christianity in public life. The revival's opponents and proponents both rejected the Puritan heritage. But neither side constructed viable, biblically based alternatives. Even more, they failed to ask how Scripture could offer guidance for getting along in a mixed culture where no one of the parties arising from the Awakening could dictate a "biblical politics" for the whole. As a result the gospel was prostituted, the church was damaged, and, finally, the spread of the Christian faith itself was hindered.

For, yes, the Revolutionary period marks a low point in public spiritual life in the country. Small renewal movements were going on in far-flung rural areas of the country.[33] But in general, the Revolutionary period was marked by declining concern for church, weakness in evangelism, and general spiritual lassitude. Not until the local revivals in Virginia and Connecticut during the 1780s, which anticipated the Second Great Awakening in the early 1800s, did Christianity show marked gains in the new United States. One of the reasons has to be that the children of the Great Awakening, though they may have gone on to adulthood in their concern for the church, had remained children, easily fooled in matters having to do with society and politics.

In conclusion, it should be clear that modern Christians need to regard links between the Great Awakening and the American Revolution with care. Connections certainly were there. And it may be possible to take some satisfaction from the way in which the style of the Awakening shaped American culture in the second half of the eighteenth century. On the other hand, it is definitely not the case that the work of the Spirit in the revival can be equated with the work of the patriots in the Revolution. At best, the Awakening influenced certain aspects of the general tone of American society in the era of the Revolution. But this influence did not necessarily lead to greater godliness or to a country with more Christians. At worst, on the other hand, the failure of the heirs of the Awakening to replace Puritan convictions about society with a biblically based framework of their own created major problems during the Revolution. Christian patriots, with no self-consciously Christian moorings to anchor their approach to politics, were swept along with the nationalistic tide. This, unfortunately, contributed to the debasement of the faith in the era of the Revolution.

Two final words are in order. First, the presentations of this chapter do not speak directly about the ideas of the Revolution itself. To this point all we have seen is that some Christians, with roots in the Great Awakening, made patriotism their idol during the War. This does not yet say anything, positive or negative, about the cause of the patriots. That is a subject which we approach directly in the next chapter.

Second, the story of the connection between the Great Awakening and the American Revolution points to an important Christian task. George Whitefield and Jonathan Edwards are two of the brightly shining lights in American evangelical history. Yet they did not accomplish everything that needed to be done. What American believers required in the mid-1700s were dedicated Christians who were just as discerning in political thought as Whitefield was in evangelism and Edwards in theology. Later in this book, especially in Chapter 6, some guidelines are suggested which might have enabled Christians during the Revolution both to preserve their faith from the corruptions of a rampant nationalism and yet support some of the political principles of the new country even if they were not drawn from the Bible.

In short, if an Edwards had existed for political theory in the 1770s—working diligently to draw from Scripture an approach to public affairs, carefully studying the wisdom of the world to discriminate between the helpful and the harmful—it is possible that the gospel would have been better served during the Revolution. The same may be said for today. The work of Christian evangelists and apologists, especially when they make pronouncements on public issues, needs to be complemented by the careful development of Christian political theory and practice by Christian politicians and theorists. The lesson of the 1700s is that without such mutual support, the message of revival can easily become a captive to one or another of the patriotic spirits of the age. And that can do the cause of Christ great harm.

THE GREAT AWAKENING AND THE AMERICAN REVOLUTION: NOTES

[1]Alan Heimert, *Religion and the American Mind from the Great Awakening to the American Revolution* (Cambridge, MA: Harvard University Press, 1966), p. 483; Richard A. Harrison, "Samuel Spring," *Princetonians 1769-1775: A Biographical Dictionary* (Princeton: Princeton University Press, 1980), pp. 167, 168.

[2]Heimert's general perspective is echoed in several influential essays by William C. McLoughlin, including "The Role of Religion in the Revolution: Liberty of

Conscience and Cultural Cohesion in the New Nation," *Essays on the American Revolution*, Stephen G. Kurtz and James H. Hutson, eds. (Chapel Hill: University of North Carolina Press, 1973); and "Religious Freedom and Popular Sovereignty: A Change in the Flow of God's Power, 1730-1830," *In the Great Tradition: In Honor of Winthrop S. Hudson*, Joseph D. Ban and Paul R. Dekar, eds. (Valley Forge, PA: Judson, 1982).

[3]Mark R. Shaw, "The Spirit of 1740," *Christianity Today*, Jan. 2, 1976, 8.

[4]John R. Price, *America at the Crossroads: Repentance or Repression?* (Indianapolis: Christian House Publishing Company, 1976), p. 227. It is worth mentioning that Ethan Allen was one of the most prominent Deists in early America and an ardent opponent of the divinity of Christ and the supernatural character of Scripture.

[5]Good studies of the Awakening include Edwin Scott Gaustad, *The Great Awakening in New England* (New York: Harper & Brothers, 1957); and John M. Bumsted and John E. Van de Wetering, *What Must I Do To Be Saved? The Great Awakening in Colonial America* (Hinsdale, IL: Dryden, 1976).

[6]See the full biography by Arnold A. Dallimore, *George Whitefield: The Life and Times of the Great Evangelist of the Eighteenth-Century Revival*, two volumes (Westchester, IL: Crossway Books, 1979), or much more briefly, the insightful sketch by Harry S. Stout in *The Eerdmans Handbook to Christianity in America*, by David Wells, *et al.* (Grand Rapids: Eerdmans, 1983), pp. 108, 109.

[7]The most authoritative writings on Jonathan Edwards today are the introductions to the several volumes of the Yale Edition of his works. Harold P. Simonson, *Jonathan Edwards: Theologian of the Heart* (Grand Rapids: Eerdmans, 1974) is a reliable study.

[8]*Op. cit.*, Bumsted and Van de Wetering, *What Must I Do To Be Saved?*, pp. 130, 132.

[9]*Ibid.* See also Gerald F. Moran, "Religious Revival, Puritan Tribalism, and the Family in Seventeenth-Century Milford, Connecticut," *William and Mary Quarterly*, 3rd ser., 36 (Apr. 1979), 236-254, for further relevant statistics extending into the eighteenth century.

[10]There were several reasons why church membership figures are so small. New England churches often required a public profession of personal faith, which was never made lightly and which could be a major trauma for retiring souls. In the South the absence of Anglican bishops, who were necessary for induction into regular church membership, made it difficult to become a full member in the Anglican churches.

[11]For the most up-to-date compilations, see Patricia U. Bonomi and Peter R. Eisenstadt, "Church Adherence in the Eighteenth-Century British American Colonies," *William and Mary Quarterly*, 3rd ser., 39 (Apr. 1982), 245-286.

[12]See Carl Bridenbaugh, *Mitre and Sceptre: Transatlantic Faiths, Ideas, Personalities, and Politics, 1689-1775* (New York: Oxford, 1962), on the role which fear of the Church of England played in the coming of the War.

[13]The following paragraph draws heavily on Harry S. Stout, "Religion, Communications, and the Revolution," *William and Mary Quarterly*, 3rd ser., 34 (1977), 519-541. For a popular version, see Stout, "The Transforming Effects of the Great Awakening," in *op. cit.*, *The Eerdmans Handbook to Christianity in America*.

[14]The following sections are a condensation of material treated at greater length in Mark A. Noll, "From the Great Awakening to the War for Independence: Christian Values in the American Revolution," *Christian Scholar's Review*, 12 (1983), 99-110.

[15]For a life history, see Glenn Paul Anderson, "Joseph Bellamy (1719-1790): The Man and his Work" (Ph.D. dissertation, Boston University, 1971).

[16]*The Works of Joseph Bellamy*, two volumes (Boston: Doctrinal Tract and Book Society, 1850), I, xl.

[17]See David S. Lovejoy, "Samuel Hopkins: Religion, Slavery, and the Revolution," *New England Quarterly*, 40 (June 1967), 227-243; David E. Swift, "Samuel Hopkins: Calvinist Social Concern in Eighteenth Century New England," *Journal of Presbyterian History*, 47 (March 1969), 31-54; and Joseph A. Conforti, *Samuel Hopkins and the New Divinity Movement* (Grand Rapids: Eerdmans, 1981).

[18]Samuel Hopkins, *A Dialogue, Concerning the Slavery of the Africans* (Norwich, CT: Judah P. Spooner, 1776), p. 30.

[19]See Mark A. Noll, "Observations on the Reconciliation of Politics and Religion in Revolutionary New Jersey: The Case of Jacob Green," *Journal of Presbyterian History*, 44 (1976), 217-237.

[20]See William G. McLoughlin, *Isaac Backus and the American Pietist Tradition* (Boston: Little, Brown, 1967); and *Isaac Backus on Church, State, and Calvinism: Pamphlets, 1754-1789*, William G. McLouglin, ed. (Cambridge, MA: Harvard University Press, 1968).

[21]See Perry Miller, *The New England Mind: From Colony to Province* (Cambridge, MA: Harvard University Press, 1953).

[22]The best study of the divisive effects of the Awakening is C. C. Goen, *Revivalism and Separatism in New England, 1740-1800: Strict Congregationalists and Separate Baptists in the Great Awakening* (New Haven: Yale University Press, 1962).

[23]See Nathan O. Hatch, "The Origins of Civil Millennialism in America: New England Clergymen, War with France, and the Revolution," *William and Mary Quarterly*, 3rd ser., 31 (July 1974), 407-430; and Hatch, *The Sacred Cause of Liberty: Republican Thought and the Millennium in Revolutionary New England* (New Haven: Yale University Press, 1977), pp. 21-54.

[24]Samuel Davies, *The Crisis*, in *Sermons on Important Subjects* (Philadelphia, 1818), V, pp. 257, 258.

[25]Samuel Sherwood, *The Church's Flight into the Wilderness* (New York, 1776), pp. 14, 15.

[26]This entire issue is discussed at greater length in Mark A. Noll, "Christian and Humanistic Values in Eighteenth-Century America: A Bicentennial Review," *Christian Scholar's Review*, 6 (1976), 114-126.

[27]Francis Alison, *et al.*, "Presbyterians and the American Revolution: A Documentary Account," *Journal of Presbyterian History*, 52 (Winter 1974), 391, 392.

[28]Moses Mather, *America's Appeal to the Impartial World* (Hartford, CT: Ebenezer Watson, 1775), p. 52.

[29]Nathaniel Whitaker, quoted in *op. cit.*, "Presbyterians and the American Revolution," pp. 433, 434.

[30]Robert Smith, *The Obligations of the Confederate States of North America to Praise God . . . for the various interpositions of his providence in their favour, during their contests with Great Britain* (Philadelphia: Francis Bailey, 1782), p. 33.

[31]Richard A. Harrison, "Alexander MacWhorter," in *Princetonians 1748-1768: A Biographical Dictionary,* James McLachlan, ed. (Princeton: Princeton University Press, 1976), p. 196.

[32]For other troubling examples, see Mark A. Noll, *Christians in the American Revolution* (Grand Rapids: Eerdmans for the Christian University Press, 1977), pp. 49-51, 70-72.

[33]See Stephen A. Marini, *Radical Sects of Revolutionary New England* (Cambridge, MA: Harvard University Press, 1982).

CHAPTER FOUR

What Should Christians Think of the American Revolution?

Almost from the first moments of the War for Independence itself, American Christian leaders have publicly claimed the blessing of God upon the United States. Statements about the country's divine origins, like those recorded in the preceding chapter or those found in the bibliographical essay, have been common throughout our history. Also, in recent years such assessments have proliferated. Books proclaim that God had a special "plan for America" which was visible in Columbus's voyages, in the Puritan settlements, and especially in the War for Independence when God providentially intervened on behalf of "his people."[1] Other media proclaim "the God-given ideals which inspired the founding fathers of this nation."[2] And countless books, pamphlets, sermons, and public speeches speak of the Revolutionary War as a blessed event which God used to found a nation on Christian principles.

These views are widespread in some Christian circles. But they do not reflect an accurate picture of the actual circumstances of the American Revolution. Such opinions are, therefore, dangerous for Christians simply because they are not true, or because they are only ambiguous half-truths. But they are also dangerous for another reason. If modern Christians promote erroneous views of the nation's past, they undermine their efforts to live for Christ in the present.

THE RELEVANCE OF THE QUESTION

At least two things are necessary for believers to be able to act effectively in public life and to present a faithful Christian witness on issues of political and social concern. The first is a wholehearted commitment to Scripture as providing general principles for every area of life. No sphere of existence—including politics—should be approached as if it existed on its own without God. Scripture and the traditions of the church, as subordinate authorities, give us general directions for understanding and acting upon the most important questions of our day, and any other day.

But second, Christians need to be shrewd in evaluating "the wisdom of the world." Much of our culture is based upon the ideas of persons who are not trying to live for God and who are not concerned about following Scripture. When Christians confront these ideas and persons, they must carefully decide what is helpful and harmful to the faith. God has shed wisdom abroad in the world very generously; many non-Christians see the specific problems of politics and society more clearly than believers. But such wisdom about the world is often intermingled with a dangerous denial of God. So Christians are required to accept those aspects of our secular culture which, in fact, are compatible with the Bible. But they are also required to combat those aspects which are not. It is damaging when believers reject the wisdom God has spread abroad in the world simply because it does not arise from someone who is a Christian, for this spurns the gracious gifts of a loving God. But it may be even more damaging when believers act as if the mixture of good and evil making up the wisdom of the world were completely Christian.

This latter danger lurked everywhere in the years of the American Revolution, and it continues to threaten American Christians. The founding principles of the new nation contained much that Christians can approve. But they also contained much that subverted the Christian faith and which flew in the face of the Bible's teaching. When modern believers fail to recognize this mixed character of the Revolution, when they write or speak of the Revolution as if it were thoroughly "of God," they do themselves and their current efforts harm. For such a faulty evaluation, especially when connected to an appeal to "get back to the godly principles of the Revolution," asks Christians to embrace indiscriminately harmful, anti-Christian commitments, along with those which are more compatible with the faith.

Historical study can show some of the ambiguities of the Revolutionary period and its thought. But examination of the historical record must be combined with careful study of Scripture, careful attention to the practices of other Christian communities, and careful evaluation of the world's wisdom, if modern believers are to take the measure of the Revolution. Because this issue is so broad, however, it will not be possible to provide a complete discussion in this chapter. Such issues as whether Christians should ever engage in military action (even against a "tyrannical" mother-country) or whether the independence of America was a historical inevitability even if there had never been an American Revolution in 1776 are important questions, but ones which cannot be treated here.[3] Rather, this chapter focuses on other questions: How Christian were the leaders of America's Revolution? What sort of criticism might Christian historians make of the Revolution, considered strictly as an eighteenth-century event? And how should Christians evaluate the principles of revolutionary theory which undergirded the War of Independence and the building of the new nation?

THE FAITH OF THE FOUNDING FATHERS

It is difficult for modern Americans to recapture the religious spirit of the country's great early leaders—George Washington, Thomas Jefferson, Benjamin Franklin, and their colleagues. The difficulty arises because these brilliant leaders, surely the most capable generation of statesmen ever to appear in America, were at once genuinely religious but not specifically Christian. Virtually all these great men had a profound belief in "the Supreme Judge of the world" and in "the protection of Divine Providence," to use the words of the Declaration of Independence. Yet only a few believed in the orthodox teachings of traditional Christianity—that, for example, Christ's death atoned for sin, that the Bible was a unique revelation from God, or that the miracles recorded in Scripture actually happened.

There were, to be sure, a few founding fathers who affirmed the cardinal tenets of orthodox Christianity. We examine one such leader, John Witherspoon, in some detail below. In addition, Virginia's Patrick Henry was an evangelical Anglican who had been influenced by the revivalistic preaching of Samuel Davies and other manifestations of the Great Awakening in the South. Some historians even think Henry gained his skill at public speaking by imitating Davies.[4] John Jay—ambassador, member of the Continental Congress, co-author of the *Federalist Papers*, first Chief Justice of the United

States Supreme Court—was, like Henry, an Anglican of decidedly evangelical sentiments.

Most of the other great early leaders, however, did not share the Christian convictions of a Henry or a Jay. Thomas Jefferson's views are perhaps best known. As an old man he summarized the basic religious convictions of his entire life by affirming that Jesus' doctrines "tend all to the happiness of man . . . , that there is only one God . . . , that there is a future state of rewards and punishments, that to love God with all thy heart and thy neighbor as thyself, is the sum of religion." For the rest—the deity of Christ and his resurrection, the Trinity, the divine authority of Scripture—these were the "*deliria* of crazy imaginations."[5] Benjamin Franklin was not as outspoken as Jefferson against traditional Christian beliefs, but he too saw Christ as primarily a moral teacher and true religion as an expression of perfectible human nature. Jesus was a good model from whom one could learn the virtue of "Humility," as Franklin conceded in his *Autobiography*. But in spite of exertions by his more orthodox friends, including George Whitefield, Franklin never went further than that in his attitudes to the Christian faith.[6] George Washington was a reserved man who did not express his inward feelings easily on any personal matter, least of all religion. Yet his faith was also deeply moral and profoundly humane, but not particularly Christian. A recent biographer, Marcus Cunliffe, sums the matter up well: "It is true that he was a sound Episcopalian, but his religion, though no doubt perfectly sincere, was a social performance. . . . He was a Christian as a Virginia planter understood the term. He seems never to have taken communion; he stood to pray, instead of kneeling; and he did not invariably go to church on Sundays."[7] Washington was a vestryman in the Anglican church, but he attended his parish church only about ten times a year in the decade before the Revolution.

The God of the founding fathers was a benevolent deity, not far removed from the God of eighteenth-century Deists or nineteenth-century Unitarians. This God had made the world an orderly and understandable place. He had created mankind with great skill and imbued him with nearly infinite potential. The men who put the nation together were sincere moralists and great humanitarians. They were utterly convinced that human exertion and goodwill could make America a nearly ideal place. They were not, in any traditional sense, Christian. What historian Daniel Boorstin, now Librarian of Congress, once wrote about Jefferson and his friends applies more broadly to most of the founders: they had found in God what they most admired in men.[8]

The question still remains: even if the great founding fathers were not explicitly Christian in their personal convictions, could it not be true that their beliefs about society and the nation reflected biblical principles? This is indeed the case, at least in part. Even if most of the founders of the country would have qualified as non-Christian "humanists" had they lived into the late twentieth-century, they did incorporate into their politics many elements compatible with Christianity. But it is difficult to sort this through. One fruitful approach is to examine how important the Bible was for the major leaders of the Revolution and for their political thought.

THE BIBLE AND THE FOUNDING FATHERS

It should not be surprising that most of the founding fathers paid some attention to Scripture, for they lived at a time when educated people in the Atlantic community had a broad knowledge of the Bible. To be sure, Scripture exerted a greater influence among the secondary ranks of the United States' early political leaders than among the Revolution's most important leaders. Many of these lesser lights were devoted students of Scripture and tried to apply its teachings to a wide range of spiritual concerns. Patrick Henry was such a one. Several signers of the Declaration of Independence—including Connecticut's Roger Sherman and New Jersey's John Witherspoon—made lifelong efforts to base their personal lives on biblical teaching. John Jay left a specific record of his views on the Bible. Late in his life he wrote that "in settling my belief relative to the doctrines of Christianity, I adopted no articles from creeds, but such only as, on careful examination, I found to be confirmed by the Bible."[9]

Jay was also one of the many from the Revolutionary generation who took part in establishing Bible societies during the early nineteenth century. It is an indication of the place of Scripture in the private lives of many such statesmen that the founding president of the American Bible Society (1816), Elias Boudinot, had also been one of the first presidents of the Congress of the United States (1782-83).[10]

By comparison, the great founding fathers were not as concerned about the Bible. Yet, unorthodox though they were, they knew Scripture far better than many modern evangelicals. George Washington and John Adams, the country's first two presidents, respected the Bible, and Adams, at least, read it upon occasion.[11] As an old man Adams even said that "the Bible is the best book in the World. It contains more of my little Phylosophy than all the Libraries I have seen: and such Parts of it as I cannot reconcile to my little Phylosophy I postpone for future Investigation."[12] During their presidential service, Washington and Adams also promoted the Bible's public exposition by decreeing national days of fasting and thanksgiving.

It is improper to make too much of such activities on behalf of the Bible, for such leaders could also make other kinds of statements. Adams, for instance, did not appreciate the new Bible societies in the nineteenth century. He once wrote to Thomas Jefferson, "We have now, it seems, a National Bible Society, to propagate King James' Bible, through all Nations. Would it not be better, to apply these pious Subscriptions, to purify Christendom from the Corruptions of Christianity; than to propagate their Corruptions in Europe, Asia, Africa and America." And he had earlier spoken of the Christian doctrine of the incarnation, and of the deity of Christ, as "this awful blasphemy" which it was necessary to get rid of.[13]

The third president, Thomas Jefferson, refused to call for national fast days, but he still was willing to contribute money to Bible societies.[14] Jefferson remained impressed throughout his life with the morals of Jesus and intrigued by the message of the New Testament. But because he could not accept the canonical accounts of Jesus as the Son of God, he twice edited the New Testament in order to remove the objectionable, unreasonable parts.[15] James Madison, to whom we will return, agreed with Jefferson, his predecessor as president, that the government should not sanction national days of prayer. But Madison paid the Bible a higher compliment than Jefferson. Rather than editing Scripture, Madison studied it seriously during an early period in his life.[16] The last of the great founders, Alexander Hamilton, both began and closed his American career as a devoted student of the Bible. In between, his public life was taken up with great political struggle and his private life was less than spotless.[17]

The conclusion must be that nearly every important person in America's early political history had extensive experience with Scripture, even if many of them did not hold to traditional beliefs about the Bible, or to the beliefs which Christians traditionally had derived from Scripture. To one degree or another, the Bible was important for America's first great public leaders. But this is not to say that the Bible was necessarily important for early American politics. We cannot make that conclusion until we examine political convictions of these leaders themselves.

The Bible and Revolutionary Politics

We would do well to ask three different historical questions to get at the relationship between Scripture and the American Revolution: (1) Did some political leaders come to their conclusions about the Revolution because of their study in specific passages of the Bible? This, however, might not be the most important question, for it is easy to abuse proof-texting, and the crucial considerations really lie elsewhere. So a second question is necessary. (2) Did some Revolutionary leaders consciously try to translate overarching biblical themes, or principles, into political theory, and then conclude that their biblical principles demanded a War for Independence and the creation of a new country? This question is appropriate for those leaders like Patrick Henry, John Jay, John Witherspoon, and Roger Sherman who were professing Christians, but it leaves out most of the other founders who were more Deists than Christians. Another, more general question is appropriate for both them and the Christians. (3) Did the ideas, or basic assumptions, of the Revolution— wherever they came from, or whoever enunciated them—fit with the ideas, or basic assumptions of Scripture? The first two questions are easier, in the sense that we can answer them by looking carefully at the published and private writings of the Christian founders. The third question is more difficult, because it involves a comparison of two large frameworks of convictions, those of the Revolution and those of the Bible. To answer all of these questions, however, we need first to describe briefly the ideology, or the popular political thought, of the Revolution.

The Ideology of the Revolution

A whole host of recent students of the Revolutionary period have reconstructed, with great exactness and detail, the thinking which undergirded the struggle for independence and the creation of a new nation.[18] They call the ideas which moved Americans to revolt and which grounded the new country "radical" or "real" Whig ideas. These convictions amounted to both a political philosophy and a moral vision. As a political theory, they were rooted in the English Whig heritage of the late seventeenth and eighteenth centuries. This tradition was committed to Parliamentary rights as opposed to absolute monarchy, to the rule of Protestant kings as opposed to Catholics, and to the traditional liberties of the British heritage as opposed to illegitimate concentrations of power.

Whigs also shared with most advanced Western thinkers a belief in natural rights, and they believed that the social contract provided the foundation for public order. These abstract theories became an ideology with Revolutionary potential when they were inspired by "real" Whig pictures of good and evil. During the eighteenth century the actual political figures who were known as "real" or "radical" Whigs remained on the fringes of British politics, but their perceptions, especially of public authority, became crucial in America. What they transmitted across the Atlantic above all was a fundamental distrust of unchecked power, whether in the grasping hands of an arbitrary monarch, in the evil designs of a corrupt Parliament, or in the ambitious grasp of a state church. Unchecked power, the "real" Whigs held, nourished corruption, which in turn encouraged unrestrained power. Let authority get out of hand, and all the hard-won trophies of English liberty, every vestige of natural right, not to speak of the very rule of law itself, stood in mortal jeopardy.

It was this powerful ideology which in the minds of American patriots transformed the blunders of Parliament into life-or-death crises. A couple of examples are worth noting.[19] At the end of the French and Indian War in 1763, the British Parliament proposed a Stamp Tax for the American colonists. Prime Minister George Grenville thought it was appropriate for Americans to make a modest contribution in compensation for Britain's efforts to defend the colonial frontiers and to aid in easing the great war debt which the mother country then possessed. A recent historian provides a summary from the viewpoint of Parliament: "In English eyes the revenue question was simple. The British debt was staggering; the American debt insignificant. Englishmen paid high taxes; Americans low taxes. Much of the British debt had been acquired defending the colonies from the French, and now the territory to guard and administer had been enlarged by the recent war. Therefore, tax revenues from the colonies must be increased."[20] The Stamp Tax projected an annual revenue of £100,000; the English debt had grown by approximately £130,000,000 during the war.

To Americans nurtured on "real" Whig thought, however, the Stamp Tax was something else entirely. The important thing for colonists was not the war debt, but Britain's power. If Parliament could impose a tax (even a small one) on the colonies without the colonists' consent, what would stop Parliament if it wished to take more and more of their property? Perhaps the arbitrary power of Parliament would reach out even to the colonists themselves, after having devoured their property.

Another example is provided by the Quebec Act of 1774, one of the last straws that broke the back of British-American relations. After negotiating with French-Catholic leaders for years after Britain acquired Quebec in the French and Indian War, Parliament finally agreed to give Quebec Catholics the right to collect taxes for education and to exercise other privileges which were customary in the Catholic countries of Europe. To Parliament, the uproar that greeted this Act in the British colonies was inexplicable. Was not the British government giving to French Quebec some of the same liberty over its own affairs which the colonists so vociferously demanded for themselves? But residents of the thirteen colonies perceived something else in the Quebec Act. To them, it represented the establishment of Roman Catholicism right on their doorsteps. And the Catholic faith represented the Inquisition, religious tyranny, and the end of religious freedom. Americans' worst fears were confirmed—Parliament cared so little for freedom that it would establish a religious despotism in the outposts of America. What could prevent tyranny moving south and east from Quebec to cover the entire New World?

The "real" Whig picture of the world provided the same categories to interpret the infamous tax on tea. Parliament's Tea Act of 1773 represented an effort to bail out the struggling East India Company. It allowed large quantities of tea to pass from India to the colonies without paying duties in England. This made it possible to aid the East India Company, and to provide tea to the colonists at cheaper prices than they normally paid, even when a small Parliamentary tax was added to the transaction. But colonists, again inflamed by the threat of an arbitrary power directed against their property, resisted bitterly. The British thought that these complaints came only from the wealthy American merchants who would lose business because of the less expensive tea provided by the East India Company. But other colonists who opposed the Tea Act did so to defend their liberties in the disposition of their property and to protest the Parliamentary advantage given, by whim (it seemed), to a great, oligarchical monopoly.

When Boston protesters dumped tea into the harbor in December 1773, grave consequences followed. Parliament enacted measures to send British troops to the colonies, to take custom cases out of Boston, and to appoint the members of the upper house of Massachusetts' colonial legislature itself. Surely, this was not excessive action to take against the lawbreakers whom the Massachusetts authorities refused to prosecute. But the colonists saw these matters differently. Again, to them, these actions represented Parliament's grasp for unrestrained power. And so they gathered arms, and began meeting in Councils of Safety. They alerted "Minute Men" who would stand by colonial rights at the least notice. When such notice came in April of 1775, at Lexington and Concord, the war was on. It would not end until Parliament sanctioned American rights, and American independence, with the Treaty of Paris in 1783. The importance of the "real" Whig politics is that this perspective governed the colonists' perception of events. Americans understood the actions of Parliament in terms which they had learned from the "real" Whigs.

Origins of "Real" Whig Politics

In recent years, another group of talented scholars has painstakingly traced the growth of "real" Whig convictions in British and European political traditions.[21] The Whig conception of politics grew out of turbulent struggles between King and Parliament during the first half of the seventeenth century. Puritan efforts, 1640-1660, to curb the monarchy and advance the cause of Parliament while perfecting the Protestant Reformation, added a note of religious dissent. Whig politics enjoyed its finest hour in the Glorious Revolution of 1688 which ousted the Catholic James II, installed the Protestants William and Mary on the throne, and called forth classic justifications of these actions by John Locke. Whig principles remained the theoretical basis for British politics throughout the eighteenth century. But even leaders of Parliament admitted that political infighting and petty grabs for power were the actual wellsprings of public policy throughout the period. Nonetheless, "radical" Whigs, who were excluded from ruling circles, continued to express fears for freedom and to contend that anticipations of tyranny were rampant in nominally Whig England. These "radical" Whigs were voices crying in the wilderness of Britain during the 1760s and 1770s, but in America they made straight the way for revolution. Their picture of the world encouraged a nearly hysterical fear in America of Parliament's corrupt power, it underlay an enthusiastic defense of "traditional liberties," and it called forth fervent expositions of "unalienable rights."

It is not easy to assess the "real" Whig political tradition, simply because it was made up of so many different people and movements.[22] Bible-believing Puritans contributed to that tradition, as did the Christian John Milton, defender of a free press. But many others added to the heritage for reasons having nothing to do with Scripture or the Christian faith. Doctrinaire republicans who detested monarchy of any kind, as well as Scottish and Irish nationalists who hated the rule of the English kings, made their contribution, as did legal scholars who wished to protect the Common Law. Broad-church Anglicans like Sir Isaac Newton, who wanted to see the political order display the same harmony as the "laws" of nature, and landowners who had gained property in the Glorious Revolution also added elements to "real" Whig thought. Philosophers John Locke, who saw the state as a potential threat to natural rights, and Scotland's Francis Hutcheson, who felt that the innate "moral sense" could dictate a just politics, contributed as well. And "radical" Whiggery also brought together groups which stood poles apart on theological matters. Calvinistic Dissenters and free-thinking Deists, as examples, both chafed under the established Church of England and called for reform. In sum, an examination of the historical elements which contributed to "real" Whig thought shows that Christian values were not a stranger to it, but also that they were not the dominating influence.

"Real" Whig Politics and Biblical Faith

The question remains, was this "real" Whig ideology biblical? Did Christians adopt it because of their study of Scripture? Did they make an effort to discern which aspects of this ideology were compatible with scriptural values and which were not?

The most influential modern interpreter of Revolutionary ideology, Bernard Bailyn, acknowledges that "the political and social theories of New England Puritanism and particularly . . . the ideas associated with covenant theology" contributed to "real" Whig thought.[23] We have already observed that the founding fathers were conversant with Scripture. And it was certainly common for many Christian patriots, especially ministers on days of fast or thanksgiving, to produce texts from the Bible to support the drive for independence.

Upon a closer inspection, these "biblical" elements in Revolutionary thought show little one way or the other. The founding fathers may have read the Bible, but explicit references to Scripture or Christian principles are conspicuously absent in the political discussions of the nation's early history.[24] As one might expect from the nature of the documents, biblical texts do not appear in the Declaration of Independence, the Constitution, or the new state charters. But conscious reference to biblical or Christian themes is also almost entirely absent from the places where it might be expected—the pamphlet literature advocating independence, the various state debates over the Constitution, and the political disputes of the 1790s. In short, the political spokesmen who read the Bible in private rarely, if ever, betrayed that acquaintance openly in public.

Where ministers or laymen did bring the Bible into play, it was usually not for purposes of careful political reasoning. To be sure, patriotic ministers often applied biblical texts to support their cause. But now, after the passage of time, these efforts look more like comical propaganda than serious biblical exposition. A few examples, from a great quantity, can serve as illustrations. In 1765 a Boston minister preached on Galatians 5:12, 13, especially the phrase, "ye have been called unto liberty." His message called on his hearers to resist Parliament's Stamp Act.[25] In 1773, as colonial laymen used political weapons against Parliament's effort to impose a tax on tea, colonial ministers used another kind of weapon. Benjamin Trumbull of North Haven, Connecticut, preached on Exodus

1:8 ("Now there arose up a new king over Egypt, which knew not
Joseph") to show how innovative actions by imperial governments
can destroy the property, virtue, and liberty of a self-sufficient
people.[26] And after the Tea Act actually passed, David Ramsay of
Charleston, South Carolina, supported the American efforts not to
use the taxed beverage with Colossians 2:21, "Touch not; taste not;
handle not."[27]

As noted in the preceding chapter, the heat of conflict itself often
turned the attention of ministers to the eschatological portions of
Scripture. In 1776 at least two New England ministers, Samuel West
of Dartmouth, Massachusetts, and Samuel Sherwood of Weston,
Connecticut, both whipped up enthusiasm for the patriots by liken-
ing British oppression to the Beast of Revelation 13.[28] After the War,
a Connecticut minister argued that Deuteronomy 26:19 ("to make
thee high above all nations . . . and that thou mayest be an holy
people unto the Lord thy God, as he hath spoken") was "allusively
prophetic of the future prosperity and splendor of the United
States."[29] Throughout the various armed conflicts of the Revolutionary period, ministers applied the "curse of Meroz" (from Judges
5:23) to those who were loyal to Britain or who shirked their patriotic duties.[30] When ministers used the Bible like this, they testified
to Scripture's importance in America generally, but they do not give
modern students confidence that they were necessarily trying to
form political action on the basis of careful study of the text.

Probing More Deeply
But this is still preliminary. After noting that statesmen did not cite
the Bible chapter and verse in the expression of Revolutionary
theory or that ministers often used fanciful exegesis in the heat of the
moment, we still do not know whether major emphases of "real"
Whig thought paralleled—or even reflected—biblical themes. The
problem is complicated by the fact that "real" Whigs and Christians
often used the same terms, but with somewhat different meanings. It
was easy to slip back and forth between the Christian and the patriotic meanings of terms like *liberty,* which makes it difficult to see
where Christian Whigs were bringing Scripture to bear on politics,
or where politics had robbed words of their Christian content while
retaining their religious force. (We have the same trouble discerning
what Christian Whigs really meant as we do with theological liberals

in the twentieth century. The Christian vocabulary remains, but it is not always clear that the traditional Christian content is there.)

Clearly, "real" Whig ideology shared some common emphases with biblical themes, particularly as these had been developed by the Puritans. For this, modern believers should be grateful. Biblical writers were suspicious of sinful human nature (e.g., Jeremiah 17:9; Romans 3:23). So also were the "real" Whigs, who held that humans have an innate propensity to abuse power, if power is not guarded by restraint. Scripture, particularly the Old Testament history of Israel, also paralleled "radical" Whig convictions by affirming a close link between personal virtue and social well-being. Both belief systems held that the virtue or vice of a population is reflected in public conditions. But this similarly also contained a difference. Revolutionary Whigs did not often speak of God's grace as the foundation for the personal virtue which must provide the base for a healthy society. They preferred to think that natural, rather than supernatural, means could ensure both personal virtue and social health.

Other bonds between Revolutionary and Christian themes are harder to assess. The Bible frequently talks about the "reign" or "dominion" of sin (e.g., Romans 6:12, 14), and "real" Whig leaders often bewailed the "tyranny" of corruption. Sometimes patriotic pictures of "corruption" merely equated loyalty to Great Britain with evil, but still the common concern about the self-seeking lust for power explains why the transition from a Puritan theology to a "real" Whig politics was often so easy.

Similarly, Scripture is filled with concern about freedom—for the captive (e.g., Isaiah 61:1), in the truth (e.g., John 8:32), or in Christ (e.g., Galatians 5:1). Needless to say, patriot leaders also made freedom a supremely important value. In this, however, we are able to see more clearly some of the tension between Whig and Christian vocabularies. The Apostle Paul wrote of "liberty" to the Romans and the Galatians, even though his hearers sat under Rome in a far more restricted political situation than the American colonists were experiencing. Thus, it would seem that patriots linked too speedily biblical and political ideas of liberty. Yet it is also true that government could tyrannize over its subjects with as much force in the eighteenth century as in the first. The example of the French absolute monarchs made that clear to people in the Revolutionary generation. Christians of the twentieth century know how difficult political absolutism can make it for believers, whether—as two examples—Christians of all sorts in the Soviet Union or (until recently) Protestants in Catholic Spain.

A final example of an ambiguous relationship between a common Whig and Christian vocabulary concerns the question of history. Whigs saw history as a constant struggle between oppression and liberty. American patriots regarded it as the battle between Christ and Antichrist. It was easy in the heat of the Revolution to transfer the terms (thus making America the cause of Christ, and Britain the seat of Antichrist). But when the bond between Whig ideology and Christian faith became this snug, it had begun to pervert the faith.

Some elements of the Revolutionary ideology should have posed more obvious problems for Christians during the Revolution. Whigs, for example, often transformed the defense of political freedom into a nearly idolatrous worship. Such an attitude also appeared often among American Christians, especially those who used eschatological language to speak of the Revolutionary War. They were flat wrong when they spoke as if the successful completion of the War would lead to the Millennium, or as if defeat for America would paralyze Christian life. The Bible is full of examples where God worked mightily with great grace in situations of less than full political liberty—Joseph in Egypt, Daniel in Babylon, Paul in the Roman world, not to speak of Jesus himself. When Revolutionary Christians spoke as if the triumph of America was necessary for the survival of Christianity, they had lost their way.

"Radical" Whigs were often also full partners in the Enlightenment.[31] As such they tended to focus on the natural capacities of human nature to build a just and healthy society, even if they also remembered the need to provide controls for human nature. And Revolutionary leaders had an immense confidence in their ability to define exactly how personal actions caused the effects seen in political conflict and public conditions. This confidence was part and parcel of the Enlightenment's belief that human nature and human relationships were open books which the enlightened could read as clearly as Sir Isaac Newton had read the secrets of physical nature. To some extent, this Enlightenment confidence is compatible with Christian faith. Christians too believe that God created human nature and human society to reflect considerable regularity. They believe, as did the Enlightenment, that diligent study of human life (individually and in society) yields genuine truth.

Yet Christians are never to forget that the laws of nature, whether human nature, social nature, or physical nature, are always subordinate to God's creative action and to his living Word. Christians in Revolutionary America often lost sight of this. They assumed that they possessed a God-like ability to trace cause and effect in human affairs. This overconfidence was one of the reasons why they lost the ability to look at their situation as it really was. The King and Parliament made many mistakes in dealing with America. They abused proper rights of the colonists. But they also provided, in spite of these evils and these errors, one of the freest environments in the entire world of the eighteenth century.

Moravians, some Lutherans, and other recent immigrants from the European continent—where real persecution and tyranny often prevailed—questioned their fellow Americans about their rabid attitudes to Britain at the time of the Revolution. Why, they asked, are the patriots so excited about small mistakes of the Crown, when the American situation is (comparatively speaking) so much better than on the continent in Europe? Patriots could only reply that they knew better. They could see that a tax on tea was the tip of an iceberg masking a crushing tyranny heading straight for America. They could tell that the effort to liberalize British rule over Quebec was really a secret effort to oppress Protestant North America. The reason they could know these things was because they shared the Enlightenment confidence, and the confidence of the "radical" Whigs, that the ways of the world in politics could be read as clearly as the words of God in the Bible. They were mistaken. And in making this mistake they sacrificed an essential Christian confidence in the sovereignty of God over the structures of the world for a belief in the sovereignty of their own ability to discern the secret workings of the political world in which they found themselves.

Key Patriots: James Madison

We are often able to make a more careful evaluation of an ideology when we look at individuals who held it rather than at the entire tradition. This is also the case when examining the Christian character of the Revolution. There are two obvious choices for such a study: James Madison, who was not only the leading constitutionalist in early America but also the one founding father who had undertaken serious theological and biblical study, and John Witherspoon, who was Madison's teacher in theology and philosophy and who was also an active patriot leader.

James Madison's associations with Thomas Jefferson sometimes mask the depth of his own religious convictions. But he was in fact sincerely, if vaguely, religious, and a defender of the importance of religion.[32] Madison's early religious experience contributed significantly to the shape of his mature life. His home encouraged a formal but heartfelt Anglicalism. And Madison was very early troubled by the Anglican persecution of Baptists and Presbyterians in Virginia. These early encounters with religious persecution provided the context for Madison's later efforts to aid Jefferson in the passage of Virginia's landmark law on religious freedom.

Madison was an eager student at Princeton under the Presbyterian stalwart, John Witherspoon, who was a champion of both Christian orthodoxy and political liberty. Madison spent several years in postgraduate study during the early 1770s, part of which was devoted to examining Scripture, reading theology, and engaging in doctrinal discussions of a remarkably sophisticated nature.[33] The Revolution, as it did for many other young men at loose ends, provided Madison with a cause and a career. He became an influential political leader in the early republic but never lost his belief in the importance of religion or the need for the state to insure its free exercise. In addition, some of Madison's most influential political writing seems to contain ideas that parallel biblical themes.

Madison's famous Tenth Federalist has been an especially intriguing document in this regard. It was published on November 23, 1787, as part of the series coauthored with Alexander Hamilton and John Jay in support of the proposed Constitution. The Tenth Federalist sought to quiet fears that a popular government with the democratic elements contained in the new Constitution would lead to disaster—either when a dominant faction clawed its way to power through mob rule or when society dissolved into total anarchy. Madison conceded "the propensity of mankind, to fall into mutual animosities," and admitted that the "unfriendly passions" of humans, especially arising from "the various and unequal distribution of property," posed a serious threat to all democratic governments.[34]

He went on to argue, however, that a large, far-flung republic, with democracy at work throughout the country in representative institutions, could overcome the evil of faction precisely because its size and diversity would prevent a dangerous accumulation of power. This was, Madison urged, the very kind of government proposed by the new Constitution.

One of the perennial points of discussion concerning the Tenth Federalist is the sources from which Madison derived its view of human nature—as both corrupt and yet capable of honorable activity. It is difficult to sort out the intellectual influences which worked on Madison, for he was a voracious reader and eagerly adapted what he read for his own purposes. Some have argued that Madison's study of the Bible, and his reading of theology with Witherspoon, made the greatest contribution.[35] And there may be something to this, for Madison's Tenth Federalist and much of his other work possesses the same mingled opinion of humanity that Scripture does, of humankind as both sinner and potential servant of God. We can look at several passages in the Tenth Federalist—for example, when Madison contended that the "latent causes of faction are . . . sown in the nature of man"—and find what appear to be the results of Christian convictions.

The historical search is complicated by the fact that Madison also drew on other sources, some of which were, at least in part, antithetical to Christian teachings. Thus, Madison had long studied the Greek and Latin classics. From Thucydides he had learned about how cruel people could be to one another in both war and peace; from Aristotle he had seen the necessity to be realistic about political aspirations.[36] Madison also knew the eighteenth-century liberal, or Enlightenment, tradition with its confidence in natural rights, social compact, and constitutional government. This heritage echoed Christian convictions about the need to restrain power, but its view of God was deistical. God had nothing to do with the moral world once he had created its general laws; people had to make-do the best they could in this world in reliance upon their own natures and with their own talent. In this perspective, Christian concepts like "original sin" were not so important as the simple, pragmatic needs of organizing a new government in a vast open continent.[37]

Madison also studied the Scottish Philosophy of Common Sense at Princeton with Witherspoon, and this perspective also influenced his thinking. David Hume, the famous skeptic who questioned miracles and traditional arguments for God's existence, had provided this Scottish philosophy with political statements about human nature sounding very much like Madison's statements in the Tenth Federalist.[38] When we examine Witherspoon's beliefs, we will see that the Scottish position was aligned with Christian values in some areas but not in others.

In sum, Madison's values—particularly his views on human nature—seem to fit fairly well with general Christian beliefs. While Madison did not have an orthodox belief in God's continuing sovereignty over the world, and while he did not necessarily ascribe the political lust for power to a Christian doctrine of original sin, he nonetheless shared the Christian's skepticism about natural morality and the Christian's belief that, in spite of the deep-seated problems of humanity, it was possible to construct a political environment which promotes justice and responsibility. In terms which we used in Chapter 2, Madison's view of human nature was not fully Puritan or Augustinian, but it did retain the impress of that earlier Christian perspective.

John Witherspoon

John Witherspoon's political ideas are even more difficult to assess than Madison's. This comes about because of Witherspoon's complicated theological and intellectual history.[39] He was born in Scotland in 1723 and served as a minister there for twenty-three years before accepting a call to become president of Princeton, or the College of New Jersey as it was then called, in 1768. In America, he labored with distinction as a college president; he gained a reputation as a learned and forceful preacher; he devoted great energies to the Presbyterian church; and he also engaged in an unusual amount of political activity for a clergyman. He was a New Jersey delegate to the Continental Congress in July 1776, where he signed the Declaration of Independence, and he continued to serve in the national legislature or in the New Jersey assembly for more than a decade thereafter. His last major public responsibility was to vote for the Constitution as a member of the New Jersey ratifying convention in 1787, seven years before his death.

One problem in evaluating Witherspoon's politics is that he seems to have undergone an intellectual "conversion" when he crossed the

Atlantic to take up his post at Princeton. In Scotland, Witherspoon was a defender of orthodoxy and an acknowledged leader of the Evangelical Party in the Presbyterian Church. In particular, Witherspoon insisted in sermons and printed treatises that God's saving grace and the testimony of Scripture were essential for undergirding social well-being in this life and everlasting security in the world to come. Such views propelled Witherspoon into the leadership of an Evangelical party which struggled against the Scottish Moderates, a group that gave enthusiastic support to the Enlightenment. Witherspoon's attacks were especially strong against the skepticism of David Hume and the ethics of Francis Hutcheson, who saw no need for Scripture or God's grace in developing moral or political theory.[40] Yet a strange transformation took place when Witherspoon crossed the Atlantic. As Princeton's professor of moral philosophy, Witherspoon was required to lecture on the principles of politics. But to guide this effort Witherspoon turned instinctively to the books of his erstwhile theological opponents, Hume, Hutcheson, and other philosophers of the Scottish Enlightenment.

The results for Witherspoon's own politics were mixed. From a Christian perspective his positive goals were certainly commendable. Witherspoon desired protection from a tyranny which encouraged personal evil and discouraged personal virtue. In the early stages of the conflict he preached a memorable sermon on "The Dominion of Providence over the Passions of Men" (May 17, 1776), in which he proclaimed God's ability to bring good out of the activities of evil men. And throughout his service in the Continental Congress Witherspoon insisted that the United States act faithfully in meeting its obligations, graciously in treating defeated armies, and carefully in protecting the new liberty gained from Britain. Much of his activity, in short, reflected a desire for Christian principles to govern American public life.

But Witherspoon was also subject to the excesses of other Revolutionaries. So firmly did he believe that resistance to Britain was virtuous that he could only equate loyalty to the Crown with vice and immorality. Witherspoon gave unfortunate expression to these sentiments in 1778 and 1779 when he wrote two vicious "recantations" for printers who had done work for loyalists, Benjamin Towne of Philadelphia and James Rivington of New York. In these "recantations," which the printers were forced to sign in order to stay in business, Witherspoon put words in their mouths proclaiming their own degeneracy in working for loyalists.[41] In his zeal for American rights Witherspoon was making the new American nation a supreme value in violation of the Christian's obligation to put first the Kingdom of God. He allowed self-righteousness to triumph over charity.

The most serious difficulty in Witherspoon's political thought, however, was not its momentary loss of balance. It was rather its frankly naturalistic basis. Witherspoon, unlike Madison, was required to lecture on politics, and so we possess written statements of his thought. They present a disturbing picture inasmuch as they lack essential elements of a genuinely Christian approach to public life. That is, Witherspoon's lectures on politics and his public statements at the Congress nowhere expressed the conviction that all humans, even those fighting against British tyranny, were crippled by sin and needed redemption. They also failed to affirm that it was God's gracious providence which undergirded political life of whatever kind rather than simply nature or human nature by itself.

Witherspoon's politics breathe a different spirit than his evangelical sermons. In politics he seems very much a spokesman for the Enlightenment. Politics is rooted, according to Witherspoon, in "conscience enlightened by reason, experience, and every way by which we can be supposed to learn the will of our Maker, and his intentions in creating us such as we are."[42] But when Witherspoon said this, he explicitly excluded the Bible from what we can learn about "the will of our Maker," at least as far as politics is concerned. In fact, he began the lectures from which this quotation comes by affirming that they were "an inquiry into the nature and grounds of moral obligation by reason, as distinct from revelation."[43] And in the same lectures he criticized Cotton Mather for thinking that "moral philosophy," including politics, needed special insights from God's grace or his revelation. So Witherspoon was left to derive his politics from nature and from natural human conscience.

Modern students of Witherspoon are in fact surprised at his rejection of a biblical basis in his political thought, because they know of his reputation as an evangelical. James McAllister, author of one of the fullest recent essays on Witherspoon's role in the Revolution, asks the question, "How large a role did the biblical revelation play in his theory of civil law?" And McAllister concluded: "The answer to the question regarding the biblical contribution to Witherspoon's teaching about the law and liberty is: almost nothing. . . . his theory of society and civil law was based not on revelation but on the moral sense enlightened by reason and experience."[44] Virtually the same conclusion appears in the best, and most recent, history of American philosophy: "It is clear that he had drunk more deeply of the Scottish Enlightenment than the [Princeton] trustees (and perhaps he himself) had supposed. . . . In further contrast to Edwards, and it seems his own earlier position at Edinburgh, Witherspoon taught that questions of morality and virtue could be investigated as a branch of science and that our duties could be demonstrated by rational and empirical means. Thus he starts his ethics, not with premises guaranteed by religion or revelation, but from the construction of human nature as learned by observation."[45]

Witherspoon and the Problem of Revolutionary Christianity
The primary difficulty with Witherspoon, and many of his "real" Whig colleagues, is not so much their conclusions, but how they reached those conclusions. Christians today should regret the way in which allegiance to the Revolution became just as important as the faith itself to some Christian patriots. But they should be pleased with the patriotic insistence upon the rule of law, upon the need for virtue in a population, and upon the dangers of unchecked power. By the same token, modern believers should find the concept of God held by patriots, including Witherspoon, deficient. The "Author of Nature" can never be the same as the God who has revealed his will for humanity in Christ and in Scripture. Yet comparatively speaking, the Revolution's "Author of Nature" provided for considerable justice. And the patriots' respect for the "Author of Nature" allowed religious perspectives to function openly in public life. These are important matters, for they are not always present in modern America where secularism and materialism have such influence.

At the same time, however, modern Christians should recognize what the political thinking of Witherspoon and like-minded Revolutionaries involved. Witherspoon did not derive his politics from the Bible. He did not think the Christian God had a specific role to play in public life, where the rule of nature prevailed. And he did not worry about assuming an Enlightenment perspective on political matters.

In itself this stance was not necessarily wrong. Christians may often profitably use theories, concepts, or proposals "from the world." They can rejoice, for example, when someone like Thomas Jefferson, who had no use for a divine Jesus or a supernatural Bible, questioned the state's control of churches, even if many of those who supported a continued role for the state in the churches included evangelicals like Witherspoon and Patrick Henry.

At the same time believers must see that the positive parts of the "radical" Whig theory were not Christian in a direct sense. At their best, they included political values compatible with biblical values. They were not in themselves biblical, nor were they drawn from the Bible, nor should they be equated with Christianity.

The natural process of reasoning which led Witherspoon and other Christians to join the Revolutionary cause represents a grave danger, especially when it is regarded as a Christian process. In terms developed by Francis Schaeffer in his early books,[46] the Revolution represented the growing power of "nature" at the expense of "grace." Admittedly, the founding fathers still were better than many modern political ideologists, for God remained a vital part of their political thought, even as the "Author of Nature." But their general efforts opened up the same pathway for nature to devour grace that has been a persistent danger in Western culture since the Renaissance. Witherspoon was an upstanding Christian person, but his political theory was more directly a product of nature than was, for example, the political and economic views of the medieval Catholic theologian, Thomas Aquinas. Witherspoon's politics was certainly more theistic than much modern politics, for he was a part of the eighteenth century where some kind of God was a widely shared presupposition. Yet in Witherspoon, the most self-consciously evangelical of the founding fathers, there is little of the effort which marked the work of earlier Christian thinkers to ground politics in specifically Christian propositions. Augustine, Thomas Aquinas, John Calvin, John Knox, and (after Witherspoon's day) Abraham Kuyper in the Netherlands all tried to develop political theory which reflected the truths of Scripture as well as the natural constitution of human beings and society. But Witherspoon and his fellow patriots did not. Witherspoon remains valuable as an example of courageous activity by a Christian in public life. And many of the specific principles which he supported may still be supported by Christians. But it would be foolish to believe that the way in which Witherspoon reasoned about politics should ever serve as a model for Christian political thought.

With another vocabulary, it is clear that Witherspoon's approach to politics opened the door to secularization. His *approach*, though not his *conclusions*, was as humanistic as anything in the eighteenth-century Enlightenment, from which arose the "secular humanism" of our own day. The British sociologist David Martin has well described how secularization begins: "The key word is differentiation, meaning the splitting off of sectors, so that religion becomes one specific sector, not the essence of the whole. . . . Above all the casing of thought ceases to be theological. Philosophy is naturalised and becomes natural philosophy and sub-divides yet again into moral philosophy and other branches. Law finds a justification in social necessity rather than divine edict. Morals seek a foundation in rules of reciprocity and a calculus of happiness. The state appeals to the voice of the people rather than the voice of God."[47] This is exactly the process underway in the Revolutionary period. It describes precisely the ideas which Witherspoon communicated to his students at Princeton, but it also marks the thinking of others, like Madison, who also had a Christian background. Patriotic thought, even when expressed by Christians like Witherspoon, was proceeding on its own. It was independent from the "casing" of Christian doctrine or the Bible.

A present danger flows directly from the activities of patriots like Witherspoon. Contemporary evangelicals often fail to recognize that the American political tradition is a mixed heritage. It contains much that comports well with biblical faith. But it also contains the seed of secularization which has led to so many problems in American public life. The call for evangelicals to be involved in public action for Christ in the late twentieth century must involve, as even a minor part of the effort, a repudiation of the nature-grace confusions of the late eighteenth century. One of the reasons evangelicals are confused as they enter the political arena today is that they are not self-critical about a political tradition which, for all its good parts, has never been a distinctly Christian one. As Christians, we should not condemn the "real" Whig thought of the Revolution as pagan. But we should not entertain romantically unrealistic opinions about its Christian character. Secular processes were at work in the ideology of the patriots, and Christians like Witherspoon encouraged those processes. This secularism has had negative results, even if many of the positive accomplishments of the Revolution have served Christians, and all citizens, very well. To be better witnesses for Christ in modern America, however, evangelicals must realize why the political system is now thoroughly secularized. If we understand our history properly, we will have to join Pogo, the comic strip character, in saying that we have met the enemy, and it is us.

In sum, the thought of the Revolution was not itself Christian. This is not to say that it lacked elements in harmony with Christian faith, for there were many. Nonetheless, the Revolution marked an advance of secularization. Christians contributed directly to this secularization, especially when they identified the Revolutionary ideology, which grounded law and governmental institutions on *nature*, with the *revealed* will of God. In the eighteenth century, to be sure, nature and God were linked together, but later on the culture's view of nature eliminated God. When this happened, evangelicals found themselves without a basis from which to analyze and combat the new secularism, for they too had agreed that a good politics and a just society could arise merely from the study of nature. In the belief that natural reasoning and God would stay together, they married the political spirit of the eighteenth century; one hundred years later they found themselves widowed, clinging to a nature which the larger culture had decided could get along very well without God. Christians, to our very day, have continued to express the fundamentally misplaced hope that a nation founded upon *nature* could come back to its *Christian* home. But since there had never been a genuinely Christian home, the desire for return promotes only nostalgic myth-making and contemporary confusion.

When Christians realize the mixed legacy of the Revolution, they do not have to condemn it out of hand. But if they would avoid both the mistaken loyalty of "real" Whig patriots, who sought first the American cause and its righteousness, and the naturalistic tendencies of "real" Whig thought, which set America's hand to a secular plow from which it has never looked back, they must perceive the differences, as well as the similarities, between their Christian faith and the ideals of the Revolution.

We have engaged in a lengthy inquiry concerning Revolutionary thought. It is time now to climb down from the clouds and examine more practical matters. What about the event of the Revolution itself, rather than its ideology? Why might evangelical historians today raise questions about the Christian character of the Revolution?

WAS THE REVOLUTION CHRISTIAN?

There are two considerations which raise serious questions about whether or not the Revolution can rightly be regarded as Christian. The first is that the War for Independence was not a "just war" as traditionally defined by the Church, and hence that it was not worthy of unqualified Christian support. The second is that the patriots were so hypocritical that they forfeited whatever Christian approval their theoretical justifications might otherwise merit. Both matters are treated briefly here, even though they may be as important as the actual content of Revolutionary ideology.

Just War?

Christian theories of a just war have existed since the time of Constantine in the fourth century. They received their first definitive formulation from Augustine in the early fifth century. Wars, to be just, must be fought under established governments, they must restore justice or preserve peace, they must be a last resort after exhausting peaceful means to solve a conflict, and they must be fought with the minimum of violence necessary and with proper safeguards for noncombatants. With these criteria, can the American Revolution be called a just war?[48]

The greatest difficulties in defending the American Revolution concern whether it was fought to establish justice and whether the desperate remedy of war was required by the situation. The Americans' primary complaint against Britain was that Parliament taxed the colonists without their consent through representatives in that legislative body. The colonists, further, bridled when Parliament decreed in 1766, as a result of the Stamp Act controversy, that the King sitting in Parliament had "full power and authority to make laws and statutes of sufficient force and validity to bind the colonies and people of *America,* subjects of the crown of *Great Britain,* in all cases whatsoever."[49] This was proof positive, many patriots thought, that Parliamentary taxation was but the first step toward the actual subjugation of the colonies.

When we strip away the rhetoric, however, we are left with a much less desperate situation. Congress, in the Declaration of Independence, accused George III of a whole list of atrocities. The King had "refused his assent to laws [of the colonial assemblies], the most wholesome and necessary for the public good," he had "dissolved representative houses repeatedly, for opposing, with manly firmness, his invasions of the rights of the people," and on and on through specific allegations of royal misconduct. Each of the charges was based on real incidents of strife between the colonies and the mother country, usually during the fifteen years preceding 1776. But all of them exaggerated greatly the intent of the King and the Parliament to destroy the liberties of the colonies and the actual damages which their conduct had caused. We gain perspective on the plight of the colonists when we realize that they enjoyed more freedom than almost any region in the world in 1776. They had as many rights under the British government as citizens of Puerto Rico or Washington, D. C. (who are also taxed without voting representation in Congress) enjoy under the United States government today. Their situation was far better than that of the French who revolted against their King in 1789 or the Russians who dethroned the Czar in 1917. And it was far better than the situation faced by the citizenries of many governments today, whether Communist in Europe, military in South America, or oligarchical in Africa.

Most historians of the Revolution concede that Parliament was committing serious errors. It was making mistakes of judgment and errors in action. Its leaders, like Lord North under whom the War began, did not understand life in North America well. But virtually no historian believes that the blunders of Parliament constituted the threat the colonists thought they did. Regardless of how the patriots perceived it, they were not in a desperate situation. "In short," as historian Gordon S. Wood has recently written, "the eighteenth-century colonists were freer, had less inequality, were more prosperous and less burdened with cumbersome feudal restraints than any other part of mankind in the eighteenth century, and more important they knew it."[50]

Why then did they act as they did? Why did they resort to armed violence when a long Christian tradition had condemned the unjustified use of force to settle such conflicts? The answer can only be one of two things. The patriots had, perhaps, already come to the conscious or unconscious decision that the colonies should be independent, and then published propaganda to justify their prior decision. Or more likely, since patriot leaders were honorable men, they overestimated their ability to discern connections between Parliamentary actions and Parliamentary intentions. But, as suggested above, this confidence stemmed from an Enlightenment view of the world which had scant room for God or his revelation. In either case, it is difficult to see how Christians can without qualification defend the innate justice of the war.

The Question of Hypocrisy

A related, and even more troubling, issue provides reason for concern to Christians who wish to evaluate the Revolution. A very good book, *American Slavery, American Freedom,* by the United States' best living historian of early America, Edmund S. Morgan, begins with a succinct illustration of the problem.[51] In 1756 Virginians, as citizens of Great Britain, rallied to fight the French. To inspire them the Rev. Samuel Davies preached a forceful sermon in which he asked his hearers, with reference to "Indian savages and French Papists": "Can you bear the thought that Slavery should clank her Chain in this Land of Liberty?" But when Davies spoke these words, two-fifths of Virginia's own population was enslaved by "Protestants and Britons." Twenty years later George Washington prepared for battle once more, this time against Great Britain. He was troubled that Parliament had created a situation where the choice for America was now "either to be drenched with Blood, or inhabited by Slaves." When he wrote these words, Washington owned 153 black slaves, a number which grew to 277 by the time of his death in 1799. His colleague Thomas Jefferson, author of the Declaration of Independence with its stirring words about "unalienable rights . . . [of] life, liberty, and the pursuit of happiness," possessed about 200 slaves.

The issue can be stated simply: How can Christians look favorably on a Revolution, supposedly fought for liberty, whose leaders held slaves? To be sure, this is not simply a one-dimensional problem. Hypocrisy abounded in the Revolution. Patriots showed great concern about British assaults upon the freedom of the press, a concern eventually reflected in the protections of the Constitution's First Amendment. Yet they regularly deprived their opponents of the same freedom they asked for themselves. This problem is a particularly sharp one for modern Christians inasmuch as one of the most important presses destroyed by patriots in the 1770s, for publishing Loyalist literature, was the print shop of the Sauer family in Philadelphia. The Sauers throughout colonial history had pioneered in printing the Bible and other evangelical literature for German-speaking residents of North America.[52] There were other inconsistencies as well—for example, the fact that patriots blasted Parliament in 1774 for establishing the "tyrannical" Catholic faith in Quebec at the same time that they were writing to the Quebec Catholics asking them to join in the struggle against Great Britain.

But just as the great moral problem of British colonization was "Christian" destruction of the Indians, so the great moral problem of the Revolution was the continuation of slavery. Outside commentators in the 1770s and afterwards were quick to point out this hypocrisy. Samuel Johnson, England's profound Christian moralist, asked publicly in 1775: "If slavery [stemming from Parliament's action] be thus fatally contagious, how is it that we hear the loudest yelps for liberty among the drivers of negroes?"[53] John Wesley, who like Johnson was critical of some Parliamentary actions toward the colonists, yet made the same criticism. He republished an attack by Johnson on the colonial notion that "taxation without representation is tyranny," and noted in passing that he himself was the subject of "tyranny" since he did not meet the required property qualifications to vote for Parliament. And like Johnson, he pointedly reminded the Americans that the ones who were suffering the greatest loss of liberty were the slaves held by the Americans.[54] In the chapter on the Great Awakening we have seen that some of Jonathan Edwards's closest associates made the same sort of complaints about slavery in America, even though they were themselves patriots.

It is appropriate to allow a black leader, Frederick Douglass, to state the issue most fully. Douglass was born into slavery in 1817. He eventually escaped to the North where he worked energetically for abolition and where he eventually became a widely respected statesman. In 1852 the Ladies' Anti-Slavery Society of Rochester, New York, invited him to give the public oration on Independence Day. The following is a portion of one of the most memorable discourses in the entire history of the United States:

What, to the American slave, is your 4th of July? I answer; a day that reveals to him, more than all other days in the year, the gross injustice and cruelty to which he is the constant victim. To him, your celebration is a sham; your boasted liberty, an unholy license; your national greatness, swelling vanity; your sounds of rejoicing are empty and heartless; your denunciation of tyrants, brass frocked impudence; your shouts of liberty and equality, hollow mockery; your prayers and hymns, your sermons and thanksgivings, with all your religious parade and solemnity, are, to him, mere bombast, fraud, deception, impiety, and hypocrisy—a thin veil to cover up crimes which would disgrace a nation of savages. There is not a nation on the earth guilty of practices more shocking and bloody than are the people of the United States, at this very hour. . . . You boast of your love of liberty, your superior civilization, and your pure Christianity, while the whole political power of the nation . . . is solemnly pledged to support and perpetuate the enslavement of three millions of your countrymen. . . . You can bare your bosom to the storm of British artillery to throw off a three-penny tax on tea; and yet wring the last hard-earned farthing from the grasp of the black laborers of your country. You profess to believe "that, of one blood, God made all nations of men to dwell on the face of all the earth"[Acts 17:26], and hath commanded all men, everywhere, to love one another; yet you notoriously hate (and glory in your hatred) all men whose skins are not colored like your own. . . . The existence of slavery in this country brands your republicanism as a sham, your humanity as a base pretense, and your Christianity as a lie.[55]

It is difficult to stand in the face of Douglass's argument. The most that can be said is that the Revolution itself did encourage convictions which eventually undercut the slave system which the Revolutionaries defended. Although the principles of the Declaration of Independence did not lead its author, Jefferson, to free his own slaves, it did aid Lincoln to take that step for the nation many years later, and it has encouraged blacks to insist upon being included in the distribution of American rights. Nonetheless, it is still difficult to accept, in Samuel Hopkins's words, "the shocking, the intolerable inconsistence! . . . this gross, barefaced, practiced inconsistence . . . of holding these our brethren in slavery; and in these circumstances [during a Revolution for "freedom"] the crime of persisting in it becomes unspeakably greater and more provoking in God's sight."[56]

Christians, in sum, might rejoice in much of the Revolutionary heritage. But when they recognize how deeply the denial of freedom, a denial involving unspeakably more evil than the blunders of Parliament, was interwoven into the lives and thinking of the founding fathers, it should become impossible to call the Revolution "Christian."[57] Only careful dissection of the Revolutionary legacy can save some of its elements for the fruitful use of believers.

THE REVOLUTION, AMERICAN HISTORY, AND THE EVANGELICAL TASK TODAY

The key to understanding the American Revolution is balance. The Revolution was not Christian, but it stood for many things compatible with the Christian faith. It was not biblical, though many of its leaders respected Scripture. It did not establish the United States on a Christian foundation, even if it created many commendable precedents. Its early leaders did not see the reality of their own situation (concerning both differences with Britain and the absence of liberty in the colonies), even though they were men of extraordinary courage and exemplary personal morality.

Throughout American history Christians have usually not been able to achieve a balance in assessing the Revolution. Many have treated it as a thoroughly Christian event. But this has harmed both Christian thought and Christian action. Christians rightly aspire to be salt and light in the world and to counteract the evil of their day. But mistaken views of history frustrate, rather than aid, the fulfillment of these aspirations.

The current concern about abortion-on-demand illustrates these problems. Opposition to such practice is sometimes based on a questionable view of American traditions. Abortion-on-demand, it is said, violates the heritage of American respect for life and for the legal status of all persons. There is some truth to this, but only some. A realistic view of American history, especially the history of the Revolution, shows that from the beginning of the country, high ideals of liberty for all existed side by side with the systematic denial of legal protection for entire classes of human beings. American governments have never done a good job of protecting the powerless and the unrepresented. Even the Constitution, which often reflects sound views on the restraint of power, treated slaves as less than human and completely avoided the question of their rights. And it did nothing to improve the legal standing of native American Indians. The Supreme Court's *Dred Scott* decision of 1857, which classed slaves as the private property of their masters (an argument nearly identical to a main contention of the "prochoice" faction), was based squarely on that Constitution. Believers only harm their present efforts to witness for Christ on issues like abortion if they assume that the early history of the United States supports them without reservation.

This is not to say that arguments on questions like abortion should avoid the precedents of American history. Rather, Christians must analyze that history with care and wisdom. They must not think that it contains by itself the proper moral guidelines for today or that its traditions necessarily reinforce the values of Scripture. Believers do well to press the government for reform on issues like abortion. But they should realize that for the United States to defend the innocent victims of abortion would represent both a break with precedents stretching back to the Revolution as well as a fulfillment of ideas outlined in the Bill of Rights but nonetheless wrongly denied to whole classes of people during the nation's first century of existence.

Failure to make these kinds of critical distinctions about the American heritage has led to long-term, deeply rooted problems for Christians in the United States. In American history believers have had difficulty in creating strong and distinctly Christian institutions, especially businesses, labor unions, and universities. In addition, they have not felt it necessary to promote specifically Christian thinking on politics, philosophy, economics, law, and other concerns of the wider culture. Such thinking by its nature would accentuate the differences between biblical values and the ideas prevailing in that wider culture, especially those ideas which have only a vague religiosity. Without this consciousness of Christian distinctions it has been easy to expect the state to perform functions which belong more properly to Christian families and to the churches. The lack of strong Christian institutions in America is at least partly the consequence of assuming that the common culture, growing out of a "God-blessed" Revolution, was basically Christian. Believers have assumed too readily that "public" institutions could discharge Christian responsibilities. And this is the legacy of the age of Witherspoon when believers uncritically designated as "Christian" a complex intermixture of secular, prudential, and biblical values.

The result has been a compound problem. Christian institutions are weak because they have never sorted out clearly the ways in which they should and should not agree with American traditions. (As an example, the absence of a first-rate Christian university in America can be explained by the persistent belief that the great secular universities somehow meet the churches' entire need for advanced higher education.) But Christian support of public institutions is also damaged because believers do not see the necessity for providing genuinely neutral services in a pluralistic society. (As an example, it is difficult to see how prayer in public schools could ever be meaningful if it were to be used by adherents of all the Christian and Jewish bodies, by atheists, and by members of non-Western religions.) America is not a Christian country, nor has it ever been one. Failure to recognize this means that Christians rely on the state to do tasks which rightfully belong to Christian institutions, but that they are offended when public institutions refuse to follow the advice of the churches.

The last word on the subject must be words from Scripture. Because of what the apostle says about respecting (Romans 13:1-7) and praying for (1 Timothy 2:1, 2) our governments and our national leaders, we may as Christians have a high regard for our country and its heritage. But we may not, in the words of the Psalmist (118:9), "put confidence in princes" instead of taking "refuge in the Lord."

WHAT SHOULD CHRISTIANS THINK OF THE AMERICAN REVOLUTION?: NOTES

[1]The particular quotations here are from Peter Marshall and David Manuel, *The Light and the Glory* (Old Tappan, NJ: Revell, 1977).

[2]Advertisement for a film, *Christianity Today*, Feb. 4, 1983, p. 53.

[3]It is important to note, however, that during the Revolution itself the groups which made the most explicit use of Scripture were those which denied the propriety of warfare entirely. As an example, Massachusetts Quakers quoted from Matthew 5:44, 2 Corinthians 10:3, Ephesians 6:13, 2 Corinthians 10:4, James 4:1, and John 18:36, in one of their petitions to the patriot Assembly, concerning the release of Friends who had been imprisoned for refusing to bear arms. See Arthur J. Mekeel, "New England Quakers and Military Service in the American Revolution," in *Children of Light*, Howard H. Brinton, ed. (New York: Macmillan, 1938), pp. 258, 259 for

these references. Other biblical material used by pacifists is discussed in Mekeel, *The Relation of the Quakers to the American Revolution* (Washington, D.C.: University Press of America, 1979); the chapter entitled "The Pacifist Response," in Mark A. Noll, *Christians in the American Revolution* (Grand Rapids: Eerdmans for the Christian University Press, 1977), pp. 123-147; and Peter Brock, *Pacifism in the United States: From the Colonial Era to the First World War* (Princeton: Princeton University Press, 1968).

[4]See Charles L. Cohen, "The 'Liberty or Death' Speech: A Note on Religion and Revolutionary Rhetoric," *William and Mary Quarterly*, 3rd ser., 38 (Oct. 1981), 702-717.

[5]See the discussion in Charles Mabee, "Thomas Jefferson's Anti-Clerical Bible," *The Historical Magazine of the Protestant Episcopal Church*, 48 (Dec. 1979), 473-481.

[6]See Melvin H. Buxbaum, *Benjamin Franklin and the Zealous Presbyterians* (University Park: Pennsylvania State University Press, 1975).

[7]Marcus Cunliffe, *Washington: Man and Monument* (New York: New American Library, 1958), p. 60. For a full account, see Paul F. Boller, Jr., *George Washington and Religion* (Dallas: Southern Methodist University Press, 1963).

[8]Daniel J. Boorstin, *The Lost World of Thomas Jefferson* (New York: Henry Holt, 1948).

[9]From George Pellew, *John Jay* (Boston: Houghton Mifflin, 1890), p. 310.

[10]George Adams Boyd, *Elias Boudinot: Patriot and Statesman, 1740-1821* (Princeton: Princeton University Press, 1952), pp. 106, 259.

[11]For an account of Washington's lack of interest in Scripture, see *op. cit.*, Boller, *George Washington and Religion*, pp. 39-43.

[12]*The Adams-Jefferson Letters*, Lester J. Cappon, ed., two volumes (Chapel Hill: University of North Carolina Press, 1959), II, p. 412.

[13]Quotations are from letters which Adams wrote to Jefferson, as cited by Henry F. May, *The Enlightenment in America* (New York: Oxford, 1976), pp. 335, 280.

[14]*The Writings of Thomas Jefferson*, A. A. Lipscomb, ed. (Washington, D.C.: Thomas Jefferson Memorial Association, 1905-1907), XIV, p. 14.

[15]*Op. cit.*, Mabee, "Thomas Jefferson's Anti-Clerical Bible."

[16]Ralph L. Ketcham, "James Madison and Religion—A New Hypothesis," *Journal of the Presbyterian Historical Society*, 38 (June 1960), pp. 72, 73.

[17]Douglass Adair and Marvin Harvey, "Was Alexander Hamilton a Christian Statesman?" in *Fame and the Founding Fathers: Essays by Douglass Adair*, Trevor Colbourn, ed. (New York: Norton, 1974), pp. 141-159.

[18]See especially Bernard Bailyn, *The Ideological Origins of the American Revolution* (Cambridge, MA: Harvard University Press, 1967); and Gordon S. Wood, *The Creation of the American Republic, 1776-1787* (Chapel Hill: University of North Carolina Press, 1969).

[19]A fuller account of the contrasting perceptions of the events which led to the War, based in large part on the sources in Note 18, may be found in *op. cit.*, Noll, *Christians in the American Revolution*, pp. 15-27.

[20]Charles W. Akers, *Called unto Liberty: A Life of Jonathan Mayhew* (Cambridge, MA: Harvard University Press, 1964), p. 198.

²¹The crucial study here is Caroline Robbins, *The Eighteenth-Century Commonwealthman: Studies in the Transmission, Development and Circumstance of English Liberal Thought from the Restoration of Charles II until the War with the Thirteen Colonies* (Cambridge, MA: Harvard University Press, 1959).

²²These are sketched in *ibid.*, pp. 7-16.

²³*Op. cit.*, Bailyn, *Ideological Origins of the American Revolution*, p. 32.

²⁴The one exception was the historic peace churches—Mennonites, Quakers, Church of the Brethren, and (to a lesser extent) Moravians; see Note 3 above.

²⁵Bernard Bailyn, "Religion and Revolution: Three Biographical Studies," *Perspectives in American History*, 4 (1970), 113, 140-143.

²⁶Benjamin Trumbull, *A Discourse, Delivered at the Anniversity Meeting of the Freemen of the Town of New-Haven* (New Haven: Thomas & Samuel Green, 1773).

²⁷Wesley Frank Craven, "David Ramsay," in *Princetonians 1748-1768: A Biographical Dictionary*, James McLachlan, ed. (Princeton: Princeton University Press, 1976), p. 518.

²⁸Nathan O. Hatch, *The Sacred Cause of Liberty: Republican Thought and the Millennium in Revolutionary New England* (New Haven: Yale University Press, 1977), p. 87.

²⁹Ezra Stiles, "The United States Elevated to Glory and Honor" (1783), in *The Pulpit of the American Revolution*, John Wingate Thornton, ed. (Boston: Gould & Lincoln, 1860), p. 403.

³⁰For a full discussion of the "curse of Meroz," see Alan Heimert, *Religion and the American Mind from the Great Awakening to the Revolution* (Cambridge, MA: Harvard University Press, 1966), pp. 332-334, 500-509.

³¹For an excellent discussion of the way in which Revolutionary thinking exemplified patterns of the Enlightenment, see Gordon S. Wood, "Conspiracy and the Paranoid Style: Causality and Deceit in the Eighteenth Century," *William and Mary Quarterly*, 39 (July 1982), 401-441.

³²*Op. cit.*, Ketcham, "James Madison and Religion," p. 67; Irving Brant, *James Madison: The Virginia Revolutionist, 1751-1780* (Indianapolis: Bobbs-Merrill, 1941), pp. 112-119.

³³See, for example, the sophisticated statement of Jonathan Edwards's position on the freedom of the will in *The Papers of James Madison. Vol. I: 16 March 1751—16 December 1779*, William T. Hutchinson and William M. E. Rachal, eds. (Chicago: University of Chicago Press, 1962), pp. 194-212, 253-257.

³⁴*The Federalist by Alexander Hamilton, James Madison, and John Jay*, Benjamin Fletcher Wright, ed. (Cambridge, MA: Harvard University Press, 1961), p. 131.

³⁵This case is made well by James H. Smylie, "Madison and Witherspoon: Theological Roots of American Political Thought," *The Princeton University Library Chronicle*, 22 (Spring 1961), 118-132.

³⁶Ralph L. Ketcham, "James Madison and the Nature of Man," *Journal of the History of Ideas*, 19 (Jan. 1958), 62-76.

³⁷Marvin Meyers, ed., *The Mind of the Founder: Sources of the Political Thought of James Madison* (Indianapolis: Bobbs-Merrill, 1973), pp. xix, xxiii.

[38]Douglass Adair, " 'That Politics May Be Reduced to a Science': David Hume, James Madison, and the Tenth Federalist," in *op. cit.*, *Fame and the Founding Fathers*, pp. 93-106.

[39]For the fullest biography of Witherspoon, see Lansing Varnum Collins, *President Witherspoon*, two volumes (Princeton: Princeton University Press, 1925). The most perceptive study of Witherspoon's thought is found in Douglas Sloan, "The Scottish Enlightenment Comes to Princeton: John Witherspoon," in his *The Scottish Enlightenment and the American College Ideal* (New York: Teacher's College Press, 1971), pp. 104-145.

[40]For an example of such an attack, John Witherspoon, "Ecclesiastical Characteristics" (1753), in *The Works of the Rev. John Witherspoon*, four volumes (Philadelphia: William W. Woodward, 1802), III, 199-261.

[41]Timothy M. Barnes and Robert M. Calhoon, "Moral Allegiance: John Witherspoon and the Recantations of James Rivington and Benjamin Towne," unpublished paper.

[42]Witherspoon, "Lectures on Moral Philosophy," in *op. cit.*, *Works*, III, p. 388.

[43]*Ibid.*, III, p. 367.

[44]James L. McAllister, "John Witherspoon: Academic Advocate for American Freedom," in *A Miscellany of American Christianity*, Stuart C. Henry, ed. (Durham, NC: Duke University Press, 1963), pp. 217, 218.

[45]Elizabeth Flower and Murray G. Murphey, *A History of Philosophy in America*, two volumes (New York: G. P. Putnam's Sons, 1977), I, pp. 233, 234.

[46]Francis A. Schaeffer, *Escape from Reason* (Downers Grove, IL: InterVarsity Press, 1968), and *The God Who Is There* (Downers Grove, IL: InterVarsity Press, 1968).

[47]David Martin, "General Tendencies and Historical Filters," in *Annual Review of Social Science of Religion*, 3 (1979), 10.

[48]For a full discussion of this question, see George M. Marsden, "The American Revolution: Partisanship, 'Just Wars,' and Crusades," in *The Wars of America: Christian Views*, Ronald A. Wells, ed. (Grand Rapids: Eerdmans, 1982), pp. 11-24.

[49]*Documents of American History, Vol. I: To 1898*, Henry Steele Commager, ed., 8th ed. (New York: Appleton-Century-Crofts, 1968), p. 61.

[50]Gordon S. Wood, "This Land is Our Land," *New York Review*, Feb. 3, 1983, 16.

[51]The rest of this paragraph is taken from Edmund S. Morgan, *American Slavery, American Freedom: The Ordeal of Colonial Virginia* (New York: Norton, 1975), pp. 3, 4.

[52]Donald F. Durnbaugh, ed., *The Brethren in Colonial America* (Elgin, IL: Brethren Press, 1976), pp. 377-423; and Stephen L. Longenecker, *The Christopher Sauers: Courageous Printers Who Defended Religious Freedom in Early America* (Elgin, IL: Brethren Press, 1981).

[53]"Samuel Johnson: Political Writings," Donald J. Greene, ed. in *The Yale Edition of the Works of Samuel Johnson, Vol. X* (New Haven: Yale University Press, 1977), p. 454.

[54]Lynwood M. Holland, "John Wesley and the American Revolution," *Journal of Church and State*, 5 (Nov. 1963), 199-213.

[55]*Frederick Douglass*, Benjamin Quarles, ed. (Englewood Cliffs, NJ: Prentice-Hall, 1968), pp. 46-48; and for the full, critically edited version, *The Life and Writings of Frederick Douglass, Vol. II: Pre-Civil War Decade, 1850-1860*, Philip S. Foner, ed. (New York: International, 1950).

[56]Samuel Hopkins, *A Dialogue, Concerning the Slavery of the Africans* (Norwich, CT: Judah P. Spooner, 1776), p. 50.

[57]The extent to which American prosperity and its ability to exert its influence on the seas was dependent upon its slave system is suggested in *op. cit.*, Morgan, *American Slavery, American Freedom*, pp. 5, 6.

CHAPTER FIVE

The Search for a Worthy Past
in the Early United States,
and the Search Today

A premiere historian of early America, Gordon S. Wood, has recently drawn attention to the unusual situation which our last chapter also addressed. "It is one of the striking facts of American History," he wrote, "that the American Revolution was led by men who were not very religious. At the best the Founding Fathers only passively believed in organized Christianity and at worst they scorned and ridiculed it." So long as religion supported political harmony, few of them were all that concerned with *what* a person believed. Benjamin Franklin, for instance, had no use for a particular evangelical clergyman because "he wanted to make persons good Presbyterians rather than good citizens." When Alexander Hamilton was asked why the Constitution fails to mention God, he allegedly replied, "We forgot." Yet, as Wood also notes, "by 1830, less than a half century later, it was no longer easy to forget God. . . . The Enlightenment seemed to be over, and evangelical Protestantism had seized control of much of the culture. The United States, said Tocqueville, had become the most thoroughly Christian nation in the world."[1]

"The first half century of national life," another historian has written, "saw the development of evangelicalism as a kind of national religion."[2] During these years the membership of evangelical churches not only kept pace with population growth; the percentage of church members actually doubled. From 1832 to 1854 the population of the nation increased 88 percent while the number of evangelical clergymen grew 175 percent. By 1840 Alexis de Tocqueville reiterated his previous judgment that "no country in the whole world existed in which the Christian religion retains a greater influence over the souls of men than in America."[3] And whereas at the time of the American Revolution the largest denominations repre-

sented the staid and formal traditions of the Anglicans, Congregationalists, and Presbyterians, by 1850 the fervent piety of Methodists
and Baptists accounted for 70 percent of Protestant church members.

LEGENDS OF THE FOUNDING FATHERS

In view of the revived state of Christianity after 1800, it seems
surprising that Christians in the early nineteenth century had such
unabashed veneration for the Revolutionary generation. Rather than
being wary of the founding fathers, and skeptical of their largely
secular and naturalistic values, most American Christians considered
their accomplishments so dazzling that only the hand of Providence
could explain them. Parson Mason Weems, who traveled as a Bible
salesman in Virginia, received national acclaim after his book about
Washington (which went through some eighty editions) made available to every schoolboy the heroic myth of the country's father. Not
only did Parson Weems tell the story of the cherry tree, but he also
praised highly Washington's religious faith, his uncorruptible hones-
ty, and his stalwart courage. No less persuaded of the hand of Providence over the birth of the nation was George Bancroft, the best
known historian of Antebellum America. He judged the era of the
Revolution second in importance only to the birth of Christ. Of the
Constitution Bancroft wrote, "The members were awestruck at the
results of their councils. . . . The Constitution was a nobler work
than any one of them had believed possible to achieve."[4]
Even those more directly concerned about evangelism, missions,
and the church joined the chorus that identified the founding of the
American republic as a signal event in redemptive history. "The
millennium would commence in America," predicted the evangelical
statesman Lyman Beecher, where "by the march of revolution and
civil liberty," the way of the Lord is to be prepared. From this
nation "shall the renovating power go forth."[5] Only America could
provide the physical effort and pecuniary and moral power to evan-
gelize the world. "Our Heavenly Father," said William Williams in
1845, "has made us a national epistle to other lands." Even the
Presbyterian Charles Hodge, who normally made a sharper distinction between the church and the nation, fell into step with his countrymen when he wrote in 1829 that "if the Gospel is to form our

character and guide our power, we shall be a fountain of life to all nations."[6]

Even more puzzling is someone like Alexander Campbell, founder of the Disciples of Christ, who normally made short shrift of anything historical. Campbell dismissed the value of all the church's past experience since the age of the apostles—Protestant as well as Catholic. All was entangled with Antichrist. Like Jefferson, he thought no living generation should bow before its predecessors. The only history that did not draw his contempt was the "Ancient Order of Things," the purity and simplicity of the New Testament church.[7]

Yet Campbell's distrust of history made room for one other exception: the glorious events of July 4, 1776. In 1830, he declared that this was "a day to be remembered with the Jewish Passover." He had begun the publication of his influential journal, *The Christian Baptist*, on July 4, and later, after founding Bethany College in what is now West Virginia, he set its graduation day to coincide with the celebration of American independence. On one such occasion he called upon his students to imitate the work of Washington, Franklin, and Jefferson:

> A more glorious work is reserved for this generation—a work of as much great moment, compared with the Revolution of '76 as immortality is to the present span of human life—the emancipation of the human mind from the shackles of superstition—to deliver them from the melancholy thraldom of relentless systems. . . . This revolution, taken in all its influences, will make men free indeed.[8]

Somehow the work of the founding fathers had escaped the corruption that had left its indelible stain upon two thousand years of history. In Campbell's mind it was precisely the Revolution which had broken the tyrannical grip of custom.

This chapter attempts to grapple with three questions: why Christians of the early republic so idolized the fruits of the American Revolution; what implications such legend-building had for their lives; and how we might, on the brink of the twenty-first century, draw upon such a legacy so that we might better understand our own times and our place in them.

First of all, then, why did Christians early in the nineteenth century portray what were essentially political victories as events in a sacred drama? Part of the reason, no doubt, was that the American republic seemed to be such a phenomenal success. After the War of 1812 and the inauguration of the Era of Good Feelings under President Monroe, citizens of the United States were firmly convinced of what they had suspected for forty years: they enjoyed unparalleled levels of liberty, stability, and prosperity, not to speak of religious freedom and churches of unusual vitality. The good quality of life in America seemed to require special praise for those responsible for its origin, especially if, as historian David Potter argues, Americans were prone "to regard all things as resulting from the free choice of a free will."[9] If the American system seemed to work to perfection, honor must go to those who designed it. Beyond this explanation, two others will assist in trying to understand why legend-building became such a habit for Americans.

A NEW NATION IN SEARCH OF IDENTITY

Hans Kohn once observed that American nationalism began without a name, without a common ethnic identity, without a common religion, and without a single national institution older than the Continental Congress.[10] To become an American simply meant to identify oneself with a particular idea of liberty. A South Carolinian and a New England Yankee, for instance, could draw upon precious few common traditions in defining their Americanness. The United States could not even take pride in the English language. In spite of the efforts which Noah Webster exerted in his attempt to create a distinctly American version of the language, a project to which he contributed his famous dictionary and his own "American" translation of the Bible, the best examples of cultured speech still came from over the Atlantic.

Three realities about life in the early republic intensified anxiety and self-consciousness as Americans defined themselves and sought to create a viable tradition. The first was the terrible fear that the Union might not work, that sharp regional antagonisms would boil violently to the surface. Princeton historian John Murrin has argued that this concern underlay much of the rhetorical insistence that Americans were one people who shared a glorious past. In fact, American nationalism, as Murrin suggests, was narrowly constitutional and dangerously fragile:

In the architecture of nationhood, the United States had achieved something quite remarkable. They had erected a constitutional roof before they put up the national walls. Hovering there over a divided people, it aroused wonder and ecstacy. Some of the republic's most brilliant minds wrote commentaries on its virtues, orators plundered the language in search of fitting praise, and somebody, I have been told, even put it to music. But this genuine awe owed its intensity to the terrible fear that the roof might crash about them at almost any time, for the national walls have taken much longer to build.[11]

When, after 1820, sharp regional differences could no longer be concealed, the debate over what the Constitution had intended about slavery only underscored how different were the societies that laid claim to its common protection. Midwestern moderates, like Lincoln, thought the Constitution anticipated slavery's extinction; Yankee abolitionists, like William Lloyd Garrison, viewed the Constitution as a "covenant with hell" for leaving the institution intact; and Southerners, like John C. Calhoun, claimed that the Constitution firmly protected even the expansion of slavery.

If fear of regional fragmentation was one reason that Americans clung to an idealized version of the Revolutionary achievement, a second was the seething mobility that cut Americans off from the roots of family, church, and community. Alexis de Tocqueville pointed out in 1840 that in America "there are no traditions, or common habits, to forge links between their minds." In 1790, 94 percent of the population lived in the original thirteen colonies; in 1850, only about half of them did. Taking note of this movement, Tocqueville concluded that Americans, plunging into the West, were "adventurers impatient of any sort of yoke, greedy for wealth, and often outcasts from the States in which they were born. They arrive in the depths of the wilderness without knowing one another. *There is nothing of tradition, family feeling, or example to restrain them.*" Elsewhere, the Frenchman also took note of the constant, unpredictable social mobility in America: "New families continually arrive from nothing while others fall, and nobody's position is quite stable. *The woof of time is broken and the track of past generations lost.*"[12]

A third reality compounded this sense of rootlessness and fragmentation, particularly for devout Christians. This was the splintering of American Protestantism. The Age of Jackson experienced a period of religious ferment, chaos, and originality unmatched in

American history. The competing claims of old denominations, a host of new ones, and of supremely heterodox religious groups; people veering from one church to another; and the unbridled wrangling of competitors in what Joseph Smith called a "war of words"—all eroded any strong sense of religious authority. "Who of all these parties are right?" cried out a distressed Lucy Smith, who eventually would join the Mormons, founded by her son. "Or, are they all wrong together? If one of them is right, which is it, and how shall I know? The teachers of religion of the different sects destroy all confidence in settling the question by an appeal to the Bible." At a time when Americans hoped for broad visions of cohesion and stability, the religious scene, for all its dynamism, also was driving them rapidly apart.[13]

The legends of the founding fathers created by such a fluid society may have been as much a sign of the nation's insecurity, as of her strength. Given the centrifugal forces at work, it may have been easier to revel in an imaged age of heroism and common purpose than to reverse the pull of regional antagonism, to admit the reality of religious fragmentation, and to tackle those thorny issues which the founders had left unresolved as a legacy for succeeding generations.

THE SACRED CAUSE OF LIBERTY

American Christians were also especially susceptible to the lure of legend-building because they inherited a heightened religious interpretation of the nation's founding. As we have seen in Chapter 2, early New Englanders had determined that they were God's chosen people because they had such pure religion. By the time of the American Revolution, however, many throughout the colonies were making statements that America was elect because of the heights of civil liberty that it had achieved. This is a significant shift, for it made it possible to express secular purposes in religious terms, as Alan Heimert has indicated:

> In the years between the Stamp Act and the Revolution the evangelical ministry often spoke in the phrases of Sam Adams—who in 1772 explained that the religion and public liberty of a people are so intimately connected, their interests are interwoven and cannot exist

separately. Not the least of the consequences of such a blending of interests and issues was that elements of the Calvinist populace were allowed to think that they were defending religion when in fact they were doing battle for civil liberties.[14]

The following apocalyptic interpretation of the American Revolution by Samuel Sherwood, whose flaming rhetoric we have sampled before, was not atypical:

> God almighty, with all the powers of heaven, is on our side. Great numbers of angels, no doubt, are encamping round our coast for our defense and protection. Michael stands ready, with all the artillery of heaven, to encounter the dragon, and to vanquish this black host. . . . It will soon be said and acknowledged that the kingdoms of this world are become the kingdoms of our Lord, and of his Christ.[15]

Sherwood went on to attack the British as "one of the last efforts and dying struggles of the Man of Sin"; he threatened those hesitant to join the Revolution that the vials of God's wrath would be poured out on anyone who did not oppose the anti-Christian tyranny of the British.

In this context, where sin became tyranny and righteousness the realization of liberty, it is not hard to understand the heightened millennial expectations that appeared after the Revolution. In earlier chapters we have seen how Christians worked with these visions. But they showed up as well in even the most secular minds in America. The often profane Benjamin Franklin proposed that the seal of the new republic be a picture of Moses with his rod held over the Red Sea. At the time of the Revolution, the vision of America's sacred destiny remained intense but with an altered foundation. Instead of motivating men to create a Christian society, it encouraged them to bring about a revolution that would ensure the reign of civil liberty.

Between the American Revolution and 1800, the United States underwent a major religious depression, probably the low ebb of religious vitality in the nation's history. Yet in contrast to the downward state of religion, millennial expectancy during these years rose to new heights. One minister triumphantly proclaimed that the advancing kingdom had delivered "the deadly shock to the last section of the Babylonish Image. . . . It trembles, it reels to and fro, and threatens to fall."[16]

But how could ministers rejoice in the success of the kingdom when their own churches lay devastated by the enemy? Their answer was that God, in their view, had shifted his primary base of operations to the arena of nations. In the ringing success of the American republic, they witnessed a model for the coming age: "No sooner had the twenty years of our political operation built for us this political temple," the same Presbyterian went on in 1796, "than wisdom fell from God in respect to the millennial temple."[17]

This transference of religious fervor to national ideals became the heart of American civil religion. Christians began to suggest, as the Congregationalist John Mellen did in 1797, "that the expansion of republican forms of government will accompany that spreading of the gospel . . . which the scripture prophecies represent as constituting the glory of the latter days."[18] This shift greatly strengthened the American republic, endowing it with a new sense of lofty purpose. The nation rather than the church easily emerged as the primary agent of God's activity in history.

Whatever positive values may have resulted from Christians making sacred the political ideals of the Revolution, the process must also be understood as one of undeniable secularization. In a study of political theology in the late Middle Ages, Ernst H. Kantorowicz has argued that secularization occurred not primarily by a contraction of the influence of religion, but when religion was inflated to the point where it included also the body politic of the realm.[19] The supernatural and transcendental values normally residing in the church were gradually transferred to the state. Political religion after the Revolution functioned in much the same manner, as ministers appropriated religious values, imagery, and emotional force to legitimate political ideals and institutions. This process was made easier, no doubt, because no one among the scores of American denominations could begin to lay claim to functions that were universal or catholic in scope.

THE MYTH OF INNOCENCE

A Rosy-Tinted Past

The vitality of pious legends about the founding of the United States had at least three implications for the way Christians in the early republic came to think and behave. In the first place, religious patriotism cordoned off early American history from critical scrutiny. The achievement of the Revolutionary generation seemed heroic, monumental, even sacred. Few Americans in the nineteenth century ever stopped to view their forefathers as flesh and blood characters who knew frailty, compromise, and contingency every bit as much as themselves. While it may be slightly exaggerated, there is something revealing about the European traveler Paul Svinin's comment in 1815 that "every American considers it his sacred duty to have a likeness of Washington in his house, just as we have the image of God's saints."[20]

What this legend-building process involved, of course, was an emphasis upon some truths of the past along with a filtering out of others. In particular those historical pictures which were unflattering, or even the vast record of experience deserving neither praise or blame, simply vanished from sight. Citizens of the United States made much of the religious dedication of America's original settlers; they easily forgot the addiction to quick profits that characterized the settling of the South and, before long, which overwhelmed the mercantile centers of the North—Boston, New York, and Philadelphia. The consistent exploitation of Indians by land-hungry settlers was another drama rarely replayed. And while they gloried that American liberty was becoming a beacon to the world, they easily forgot that the same colonists of the seventeenth and eighteenth centuries, renowned for their defense of liberty, had been the very ones who rudely imposed chattel slavery upon English law, a tradition which had never before given it recognition. It was far easier to remember one's birthright simply as breaking the yoke of tyranny rather than as a paradoxical heritage that could account for the simultaneous development of liberty and slavery.[21]

The Engine of Reform and the Specter of Bigotry
It is important to note that in the nineteenth century the vision of America as God's chosen people also operated as a motive to vigorous action. The goal of Christianizing America stirred men and women not only to be active evangelists, but also to join in purging along with unbelief every form of social evil. In the wake of the revivals of Charles Finney, Christians intent on preaching the gospel also were behind numerous societies for moral reform: antislavery, temperance, women's rights, education, poor relief, and prison and

hospital reform. Knowing that their bountiful heritage as Americans required much of them, Christians in the age of President Andrew Jackson struggled fervently to remake every part of their society according to Christian standards. On the eve of the Civil War no evil was safe from their burning gaze.

But there is a much less heroic side of this quest for a righteous empire. In addition to broadening minds to reform, the goal of a Christian commonwealth narrowed definitions of who should be included within the American community. On the verge of inaugurating a kingdom that was essentially Protestant, democratic, and Caucasian, many evangelicals looked askance at anyone who threatened the solidarity of this image: Catholic immigrants, religious dissenters such as the Mormons, and most blacks and native Americans.

Even worse, this resentment of "foreign" elements could flare easily into open hostility or even violence. When Catholics objected to the explicit Protestant teaching in public schools, they were denounced in many quarters as subversives. Lyman Beecher, for instance, joined with Samuel F. B. Morse, better known for his telegraph, to make public a conspiracy by Catholics to undermine the liberties of the United States. In the wake of these fears, Protestants burned to the ground a Catholic convent in Boston and two churches in Philadelphia. In similar fashion, a virtual war was waged on Joseph Smith and the unconventional ideas of his Mormon followers, driving them from New York, Ohio, and Missouri, before an angry mob finally lynched Smith in Nauvoo, Illinois, in 1844.

Calling this kind of behavior a "tyranny of the majority," the observant Tocqueville noted that Americans were more tolerant than Europeans within certain limits and less tolerant outside those boundaries. Americans opened their arms to groups that could be assimilated into a Protestant empire, but clenched their fists at others. While Christian belief was certainly not the only factor in this intolerance, the idea of a Christian America too easily led believers to attempt to purify the nation as well as the church.

The Contagion of Liberty

The uncritical acclaim given the American Revolution also had a third implication. Enthusiastic about what the liberty of the Revolution could do for church as well as state, Americans seemed incapable of detecting how Revolutionary values might also alter, or even undermine, Christian faith. In the decades after the Revolution, the self-evident principles of republicanism everywhere brought into question the traditional roles of clergy, of theology, and of the church as an institution. "Venture to be as independent in things of religion," counseled one folk preacher, "as those which respect the government in which you live."[22] Common people were easily attuned to tantalizing themes of liberation, as one staunch New England traditionalist said of the religious ferment in his own community:

> Liberty is a great cant word with them. They promise their hearers to set them at liberty. And to effect this, they advise them to give up all their old prejudices and traditions which they have received from their fathers and their ministers; who, they say, are hirelings, keeping poor souls in bondage, and under oppression. Hence to use their own language, they say, "Break all these yokes and trammels from off you, and come out of prison; and dare to think, and speak, and act for yourselves."[23]

The kind of democratic individualism unleashed by the American Revolution altered no dimension of the church more than its theology. Most obvious in the fifty years after the Revolution was the revolt against Calvinism. But most notable was revolt against the accepted ground rules of theology itself. This second revolt attacked especially the long-standing Christian conviction that it was valuable for an educated segment of the church to remain conversant with the theological traditions of Christianity. And the reason for the attack was the great confidence inspired by the struggle for liberty in the Revolution, which now assumed nearly the same significance as divine revelation.

Abner Jones, a Calvinist Baptist turned Free-Will Baptist turned "Christian," makes plain the corrosive effect that popular notions of equality could have upon the old orthodoxy. He began his memoir, written in 1807, as follows: "In giving the reader an account of my birth and parentage, I shall not (like the celebrated Franklin and others), strive to prove that I arose from a family of eminence; believing that all men are born equal, and that every man shall die for his own iniquity."[24] Equality for Jones exploded the notion of original sin, that people were not morally free to choose for themselves. In this period one finds evidence of a similar revolt against each of the so-called five points of Calvinism, a revolt that had implications far beyond the importance of Calvinism itself.[25] For it was directed against the entire belief that the heritage of the church could be an important aid for the present. Calvinism, which was the dominant theological tradition in colonial America, merely happened to be the first to get in the way.

Just as notions of total depravity did not stand up well to the belief that individuals were capable of shaping their own destiny, so "unconditional election" seemed to deny that men were fully capable of determining the course of their own lives. The antidemocratic tendency of the doctrine of election emerged even more clearly in the idea of a "limited atonement," that Christ's death was somehow restricted to those whom God elected to salvation. Similarly, the concept of "irresistible grace" seemed to make God a tyrant of uncontrollable power, just that from which Americans had fought to free themselves. Finally, the focus on volitional commitment as the primary human obligation made the idea of the "perseverance of the saints," that we are sustained by the choice of another, irrelevant, if not contradictory.

In short, Calvinism was being dropped not in response to theological arguments but because it violated the spirit of Revolutionary liberty. During the early history of the United States self-evident principles of democracy persuaded any number of former Calvinists to strike out for a new faith. One who did so was the Free-Will Baptist minister William Smyth Babcock, who found Calvinism antithetical to democratic common sense. He spoke of its "senseless jargon of election and reprobation" and concluded that it had covered salvation "with a mist of absurdities." "Its doctrine is denied in the Practice of every converted soul in the first exercises of the mind after receiving liberty."[26]

This revolt meant not just the replacement of an older Calvinist system with a newer Arminian one. It was rather a revolt against theological systems in general, the whole creedal and confessional structure of the church, and the idea of God's truth being mediated by educated theologians. "We are not personally acquainted with the writings of John Calvin," two colleagues of Barton Stone, founder of the Church of Christ, admitted, "nor are we certain how nearly we agree with his views of divine truth; neither do we care." Stone himself not only rejected traditional formulations about the Trinity, but also dismissed the whole subject as irrelevant: "I have not spent, perhaps, an hour in ten years thinking about the trinity."[27]

In the early republic, popular theologies, claiming to be based exclusively on the Bible, refused to grant any value to the theological work of those who had gone before. Theological systems of any stripe became suspect, and common people came to think that one could in fact be biblical without being theological.[28] Any number of religious movements after 1800 reflect this bias toward a theology of the people, but none better than that of "the humble-farmer of Hampton Law," William Miller, who without any theological training convinced thousands upon thousands that Christ's second coming would take place in 1844.

The overriding message of the Adventist faith which Miller founded was the familiar theme that people should resist the authority of the clergy and learn to prove everything "by the Bible and nothing but the Bible." William Miller attacked all denominations for not acknowledging the right of the people to "interpret it [the Bible] for themselves." The theology taught in our schools, protested Miller,

> is always founded on some sectarian creed. It may do to take a blank mind and impress it with this kind, but it will always end in bigotry. A free mind will never be satisfied with the views of others. Were I a teacher of youth in divinity, I would first learn their capacity, and mind. If these were good, I would make them study the Bible for themselves, and send them out free to do the world good. But if they had no mind, I would stamp them with another's mind, write bigot on their forehead, and send them out as slaves.[29]

In sum, traditional theology itself, along with the riches of the Christian heritage, had been largely set aside by 1830. David Rice, the father of Presbyterians in Kentucky, characterized this prevailing mood as "knowledge consisting of fragments, scraps picked up from here and there." Whether one regards the erosion of Calvinism in America as good, bad, or indifferent is not the primary issue. The important thing is that an ideology linked to a mythic Revolutionary liberty changed ground rules so drastically that it left the American church cut off from rich sources of nourishment from the past. In time it meant that American Christians were much less able to express the gospel in all its profundity. In the headlong rush to realize freedom's potential, few Christians in America paused to consider the consequences.

MYTHS OF INNOCENCE, AND OF GUILT

Expansive myths about America's beginnings remain a deep and vital current within our culture. It was only thirty years ago that Samuel Eliot Morison could remark that the prevailing view of American intellectuals toward their national past was "a friendly, almost affectionate attitude." The first half of the twentieth century saw a rekindling of faith and pride in national institutions. Writing of the American record of leadership in Western civilization during the two world wars and the Cold War, the historian Allan Nevins could say, "It stands invested with all the radiance of the Periclean era, the Elizabethan era, and the era of Pitt and the long struggle against Napoleon."[30] Until recent times a majority of Americans identified with America's religious, if not her distinctly Christian, origins and purpose. The Englishman G. K. Chesterton commented earlier in this century that the United States appeared to be a nation with the soul of a church. The pledge of allegiance claiming that we are a nation under God, the parades and ceremonies on Memorial Day and the Fourth of July, the honor bestowed upon the American flag and the "National Anthem"—these customs and patterns were as widely followed as they were deeply held.

In our own day, however, sizable cracks have appeared in this standard interpretation of America's spiritual heritage. Particularly among the generation under forty, the American flag less often evokes the patriotic kind of emotion that borders on religious feeling; the strains of "America" no longer move an audience to solemn reverence, and eyes remain dry. Even more disturbing for those who revere America's Christian heritage is the forceful attack upon traditional ideals and institutions of the nation. Instead of confidence and pride in our past, a new generation has pictured America as almost the embodiment of evil. Turning from that which made America a refuge and a beacon, they have pointed to themes of oppression, discord and slavery. And in the aftermath of Vietnam and Watergate, influential people have ridiculed the love of God and country, unfurling a new banner confessing that they are ashamed to be American.

The most striking feature of this change is the degree to which American intellectuals—professors, writers, and other social analysts—have inverted the myth of American innocence. In the wake of the social tensions of the 1960s and the Vietnam era, a mood of collective guilt swept over educated America. Young historians, taking a fresh look at the American past, have discovered a saga of injustice, exploitation, greed, and self-righteousness. As C. Vann Woodward recently noted, the vocabulary of early America now is completely reversed: "discovery" of the New World has become "invasion"; "settlement" is now "conquest"; and what was once the "Virgin Land" is now called a "Widowed Land." The advancement of the Western frontier is sometimes pictured as genocide of the Indians, and the achievements of the Revolution are considered in terms of their excessive cost for the underprivileged and those in bondage.[31] The "glorious experiment" which called for adoration has given way to a tale of infamy which demands repentance.

Christian Reflections

Christians who think carefully about these contrasting pictures of the American past might wish to make two edifying conclusions. The first is that we need to reject simplistic and one-dimensional myths whether they be of innocence or of guilt. We should neither think of ourselves more highly than we ought nor set a standard of perfection before which any normal human activity appears unworthy. We must explore the American past in all its complexity, taking note of mercy, generosity, and freedom as well as of cruelty, greed, and oppression. Before making snap moral judgments, we must delve deeply into our past, and we must place that history in a broad comparative framework. One index of the strength of the old myth of innocence is that the current fixation on guilt is just as absolute, just as immune to balanced realism, as the rosy picture it replaces. Both myths are destined to abide with us for some time, and Christians would do well to avoid the dogmas of either.

Understanding the clash between these opposing interpretations also makes possible a second valuable insight, for it reveals how radically diverse our modern culture is. Given the influence of negative myths during the last twenty years, it is little wonder that many Americans have thirsted for a renewed confidence and pride in the American past. The current revival of legends about the founding fathers cannot be understood apart from the power of both myths—the golden one that is now almost two centuries old, and the more recent, darker one which constitutes a frontal assault upon it.

In recent years we have lived through the first generation in the history of the republic which has, at least in part, repudiated the legend of a glorious national origin and a righteous national character. Before we can regain the perspective needed to sort out history and legend, we must understand the dimensions of the wrenching events through which we have lived. We must think through what it means for people with opposite views of the meaning of America to live together in the same republic. And we must determine honestly which version of the myth colors our own judgments. Such understanding of ourselves and of our own culture may not tell us if America was ever genuinely Christian, but at least it will explain why the search for a Christian America remains such a lively issue.

THE SEARCH FOR A WORTHY PAST: NOTES

[1]Gordon S. Wood, "Evangelical America and Early Mormonism," *New York History*, 61 (Oct. 1980), 359, 360.

[2]Martin E. Marty, *Righteous Empire: The Protestant Experience in America* (New York: Dial, 1970), p. 57.

[3]Alexis de Tocqueville, *Democracy in America* (New York: Random House, 1945), I, p. 303.

[4]Wesley Frank Craven, *The Legend of the Founding Fathers* (Ithaca, NY: Cornell University Press, 1956), p. 149; Garry Wills, "Mason Weems, Bibliopolist," *American Heritage*, 33 (Feb.-Mar. 1981), 66-69.

[5]Lyman Beecher, "A Plea for the West" (1835) in *God's New Israel: Religious Interpretations of American Destiny*, Conrad Cherry, ed. (Englewood Cliffs, NJ: Prentice-Hall, 1971), p. 120.

[6]For a full discussion of this civil millennialism in the new republic, see Nathan O. Hatch, *The Sacred Cause of Liberty: Republican Thought and the Millennium in Revolutionary New England* (New Haven: Yale University Press, 1977), Chapter 4, "Visions of a Republican Millennium: An Ideology of Civil Religion in the New Nation"; also valuable is Perry Miller, *The Life of the Mind in America from the Revolution to the Civil War* (New York: Harcourt, Brace & World, 1965), pp. 49-58.

[7]For fuller consideration of Campbell, see Nathan O. Hatch, "The Christian Movement and the Demand for a Theology of the People," *Journal of American History*, 67 (Dec. 1980), 545-567.

[8]Alexander Campbell, "An Oration in Honour of the Fourth of July, 1830," *Popular Lectures and Addresses* (Philadelphia, 1863), pp. 374, 375.

[9]David M. Potter, *People of Plenty: Economic Abundance and the American Character* (Chicago: University of Chicago Press, 1954), p. 111.

[10]Hans Kohn, *American Nationalism,* as quoted by John M. Murrin, "Anglicization and Identity: The Colonial Experience, the Revolution, and the Dilemma of American Nationalism," paper presented to a meeting of the Organization of American Historians, Denver, Colorado, April 1974, pp. 26, 27.

[11]*Op. cit.,* Murrin, "Anglicization and Identity," p. 39.

[12]Quoted in Michael Kammen, *A Season of Youth: The American Revolution and the Historical Imagination* (New York: Oxford, 1978), pp. 3, 4.

[13]Quoted from Nathan O. Hatch, *"Sola Scriptura and Novus Ordo Seclorum,"* in *The Bible in America: Essays in Cultural History,* Hatch and Mark A. Noll, eds. (New York: Oxford, 1982), pp. 69, 73, 74.

[14]Alan Heimert, *Religion and the American Mind From the Great Awakening to the Revolution* (Cambridge, MA: Harvard University Press, 1966), p. 359.

[15]Samuel Sherwood, *The Church's Flight into the Wilderness* (New York, 1776), pp. 39-49. For full discussion of the themes developed in the following paragraphs, see *op. cit.,* Hatch, *The Sacred Cause of Liberty.*

[16]David Austin, *The Millennial Door Thrown Open* (East Windsor, CT, 1799), pp. 20, 22.

[17]*Ibid.,* p. 30.

[18]Quoted in *op. cit.,* Hatch, *The Sacred Cause of Liberty,* p. 139.

[19]Ernst H. Kantorowicz, *The King's Two Bodies: A Study in Medieval Political Thought* (Princeton: Princeton University Press, 1957), pp. 207-233.

[20]Marcus Cunliffe, *George Washington: Man and Monument* (Boston: Little, Brown, 1958), p. 21. On the way in which Washington was likened to a whole host of biblical figures at his death, see Mark A. Noll, "The Image of the United States as a Biblical Nation, 1776-1865," in *op. cit., The Bible in America,* pp. 41, 45.

[21]On the nature of this paradox, see the discussion of "hypocrisy" in Chapter 4, and the superb book, which that chapter uses, by Edmund S. Morgan, *American Slavery, American Freedom: The Ordeal of Colonial Virginia* (New York: Norton, 1975).

[22]Elias Smith, *The Lovingkindness of God Displayed in the Triumph of Republicanism in America: Being a Discourse Delivered . . . July Fourth, 1809* (n.p., 1809), p. 32.

[23]Walter Harris, *Characteristics of False Teachers* (Concord, NH, 1811), pp. 5, 19.

[24]Abner Jones, *Memoir of Elder Abner Jones* (Boston: William Crosby, 1842).

[25]For a more complete discussion of how the Revolutionary faith undercut the "five points" of Calvinism, see Mark A. Noll, *Christians in the American Revolution* (Grand Rapids: Eerdmans for the Christian University Press, 1977), pp. 171, 172.

[26]See the William Smyth Babcock Papers, American Antiquarian Society, Worcester, Massachusetts.

[27]Quotations and discussion from *op. cit.,* Hatch, "The Christian Movement," 556, 557.

[28]On the democratic origins of the plea for "the Bible only" or "no creed but the Bible," see *op. cit.,* Hatch, *"Sola Scriptura and Novus Ordo Seclorum"* from *The Bible in America.*

[29]For this quotation and a more extensive analysis, see Nathan O. Hatch, "Elias Smith and the Rise of Religious Journalism in America," in *Printing and Society in Early America* (Worcester, MA: American Antiquarian Society, 1983).

[30]C. Vann Woodward, "The Fall of the American Adam: Myths of Innocence and Guilt," *The New Republic*, Dec. 2, 1981, 13-16.

[31]*Ibid.*, 14.

CHAPTER SIX

Return to Christian America: A Political Agenda?

One of the most frequent themes in this volume is the declaration of Americans that their nation is like a New Israel. From Puritan New England to the popular Christianity of today rings the refrain that America is to be understood not only in the light of Scripture, but especially through the parts of the Old Testament which describe the Hebrews as God's special people.

For just as long, however, another heritage, going all the way back to Roger Williams, has questioned the America-as-Israel theme. Williams and his spiritual offspring have emphasized the New Testament more than the Old in understanding modern nations. Many Baptists, especially when concerned about separation of church and state, have followed Williams in this New Testament emphasis. Anabaptists and most Lutherans in America, preserving older Reformation traditions, also have usually refused to seek political manifestations of the Kingdom. Revivalists from a variety of heritages have urged a simple New Testament message of personal salvation while carefully steering clear of any divisive social-political issues.

Even within the more Calvinistic tradition one important nineteenth-century teaching said that America was more like Babylon than like Israel. This was dispensationalism, which eventually spread widely in twentieth-century fundamentalism and Pentecostalism, and which specifically repudiated the idea of "Christian" nations or new Israels.

It is remarkable then that, despite so much in America's theological heritage which repudiates political programs to establish a biblical nation or New Israel, these ideals persist with such power. Especially notable is the fact that these ideals flourish in some traditions where one might not expect them. So we find Jerry Falwell, a Baptist and a dispensationalist, directly repudiating his own earlier view that clergy should stay out of politics.[1] Falwell's change of heart reflects his adoption of Puritan Old Testament models for understanding Christianity and the nation. In his Moral Majority campaigns he constantly comes back to the idea of a national covenant, that the success or failure of America depends directly on her morality. So he says in a typical remark:

> I am convinced that what Solomon said in the Proverbs, thirty-five hundred years ago, is the key to our survival. He said, and I paraphrase, living by God's principles promotes a nation to greatness. Violating God's principles brings a nation to shame. The last 20 to 30 years we have suffered shame and of late, international embarrassment because we have been violating God's principles.[2]

This covenant theme, which almost exactly duplicates statements made by Puritans as early as the 1630s, is repeated over and over by contemporary evangelists. It is the basis of the 2 Chronicles 7:14 campaign which links America's repentance to God's "healing" of his "people." America, say the popular preachers, was founded as a Christian nation. She has been chosen by God to be an instrument for the salvation of the earth. Her great blessings, material prosperity, military strength, and world leadership are evidences of this special calling. They reflect also that America indeed has been a good nation. "America is great because America is good," they say, following a favorite quotation from Tocqueville. Recently, within the last generation, they lament, the glory has departed. America has turned to gross immorality, and so is declining rapidly. It is now almost too late; but we may save America if we act immediately.[3]

While these themes are far from new, they recently have gained new life as important components of a political agenda. America is to be brought back to her Christian heritage through *political* action. "It is time," proclaims Jerry Falwell, "for Americans to come back to the faith of our fathers, to the Bible of our fathers, and to the biblical principles that our fathers used as a premise for this nation's establishment."[4] Tim LaHaye concurs. Christians, he urges, must "vote in pro-moral leaders who will return our country to the biblical base upon which it is founded."[5]

SECULAR HUMANISM

This political program, in its manifestations of the 1980s, calls for warfare against the enemy designated "secular humanism." America, a specially blessed nation, has until recently been essentially Christian, according to this view. Now, however, "humanism" or "secular humanism" has been replacing that Christian heritage in America's schools, media, courts, political theory, and public life generally. "Humanism" is defined as an essentially religious faith in humanity as the ultimate source of values in the universe. As the result of the spread of this secular humanism, especially since World War II, America has turned away from its moral heritage and hence, in punishment, is losing its world leadership and prestige.[6]

This picture, it is worth pointing out, is a mixture of truth and error. Humanism in the sense defined (it can also mean a regard for the ancient classics or a concern for human cultural development, so that there are "Christian humanists") is not a unified movement. Although the *Humanist Manifesto I* (1933) and *II* (1973) loom large in the minds of the critics of humanism, these statements do not function as creeds, except for the relatively small groups which promote them. Humanism dates back to classical Greece, and has in fact been a part of the American tradition since the first English settlements. Secularism or secular humanism, especially as it was implicit in Revolutionary ideology, has always been a major part of America's heritage. Secular humanism thus comes in many forms and is of ancient lineage. Humanism, or faith in humanity, has been mixed with virtually every American religious heritage, including evangelicalism and fundamentalism.[7] Most commonly, since the nineteenth century, many Americans, including many evangelical Christian Americans, have tended to believe in the essential goodness of humanity, in the importance of believing in oneself, in self-help, and the ability of a free people to solve their own problems. When mixed with Bible-affirming Christianity, such humanism has been particularly elusive.

Recent politically oriented critics of "humanism" seldom have attacked modern faith in humanity in any consistent or general way, since their own views have contained humanistic elements, such as faith in American "rugged individualism."[8] What they are attacking, rather, is a particular kind of faith in humanity that indeed is tremendously influential in twentieth-century America. Calling this outlook "humanism" or "secular humanism," however, seems confusing; it would probably be more accurate to use the term "relativistic secularism" to describe a modern reality that is indeed powerful, widespread, and antagonistic to Christian faith.

The truth, then, in the attacks on "humanism" is that relativistic secularism is a major cultural force in twentieth-century America. Although not a unified movement or belief system, relativistic secularism involves a broad consensus of shared ideas that dominates American intellectual life, law, politics, and the media. This world view attacks all absolutes other than the value of humanity and the worth of the scientific method as the best means of mastering reality. Rather than looking for fixed truth or law, this world view begins with the premise that what we can observe is all there meaningfully is, and that change is the central motif for understanding reality. Beliefs about truth, law, or morality, accordingly, are determined by social conditions and vary in different cultures and times. Truth, law, and morality are best understood sociologically, as products of social forces. Such social determinism is balanced by a fervent faith in the value of the freedom of each individual for equal opportunity creatively to develop his or her full potential. Societies, using their scientifically based understanding of human conditions, should organize so as to guarantee such equality of opportunity while maximizing personal freedom, especially freedom from material needs. Almost every major development in twentieth-century American life, good as well as bad, has reflected the dominance of this consensus world view.

Only since the later 1970s, however, have politically oriented American evangelicals and fundamentalists characteristically focused their attacks on this "secular humanist" world view.[9] Previously, politically conservative evangelicals typically had worried about New Deal Democratic politics, the threat of communism, and growing permissiveness especially in the area of drugs and sexuality. Only in the field of education did they commonly speak of the threat of "humanism," especially in connection with their judicial efforts to ban the teaching of biological evolution in public schools. During the latter 1970s and early 1980s, however, the theme of "secular humanism," together with its counterpart, that America should return to its Christian origins, swept through American fundamental-ist and evangelical communities and became the popular ideological basis for large-scale political efforts.

The Historical Argument

For those who hold to the "Christian America" view, the situation may be summarized as follows: America was founded as a "Christian nation." But the nation turned from its Christian foundation and in recent decades has been taken over by secular humanism. The goal today is to become a Christian nation once again—by restoring America to its "biblical base," to the "biblical principles of our founding fathers," to a "Christian consensus," etc. (Typically this biblical heritage is linked directly to America's founding documents, the Declaration of Independence and the Constitution.) Stated in this way then, the only alternative seems to be an all-out battle between the forces advocating a return to "Christian America" and the ruling forces of "secular humanism"—so that America can be-come a Christian nation once again.[10]

Before jumping on the Christian nation bandwagon, however, it is important to recognize that this is in part an *historical* argument, and that as an historical argument this line of thinking contains a number of severe difficulties. In what sense can the authors of the Declara-tion of Independence be said to hold a "Christian world view"? We have already discussed in an earlier chapter the ambiguities of "Christian" as an adjective ascribed to world views.[11] Something that is "Christian" may turn out to be only generically Christian, that is, having some Christian lineage; or it may be only weakly or vaguely Christian. Certainly the Judeo-Christian heritage was an important influence, as we have already seen, during the Revolution-ary period. But there were many non-Christian influences too; and America's origins were, in important ways, a mixture of these non-Christian and Christian influences.

This is especially the case when we try to discover a *direct link* between explicitly Christian thinking and the founding documents of America.[12] As we have seen in earlier chapters, many of America's founding fathers had very minimal views concerning the fall of the human race, and almost all were highly optimistic about the capaci-ties of human reason to discover natural law unaided by revelation. Thomas Jefferson, the author of the Declaration, especially repudiated the idea of subordinating his thought to biblical principles. Later Jefferson spent spare time while he was in the White House editing out the supernatural parts of the Bible which offended his Enlightenment sensibilities.

Of course some of the American revolutionaries were evangelical Christians and did not share the extreme views of Jefferson. They, however, seem to have had remarkably little sense of a conflict between their Christian world view and the more optimistic views of human nature that strongly influenced eighteenth-century political theory. It is worth noting that even the most theologically conservative founders, like the Scottish-American clergyman, John Witherspoon, held such "humanistic" views. All people were endowed with common sense which allowed them naturally to discover the truth. The dictates of "reason" were thus the proper basis for political theory and action. So a Christian approach to political theory was only a matter of accepting the best political science of the day. Christian belief was an "option" that added other sorts of truth drawn from Scripture.[13] Whatever the merits of such Revolutionary thinking (a question we shall consider shortly), even its most "Christian" versions show little *direct link* between explicitly Christian thinking and the founding documents.

Here then is the "historical error": It is historically inaccurate and anachronistic to confuse, and virtually to equate, the thinking of the Declaration of Independence with a biblical world view, or with Reformation thinking,[14] or with the idea of a Christian nation.[15] In other words it is wrong to call for a return to "Christian America" on two counts: First, for theological reasons—because since the time of Christ there is no such thing as God's chosen nation; second, for historical reasons, as we have seen—because it is historically incorrect to regard the founding of America and the formulation of the founding documents as being Christian in their origins. Yet this error is one of the most powerful ideas of our day; and on this confusion rest many of the calls to make war on secular humanism and to "restore" the Bible as the sole basis for American law and government.[16]

The Declaration of Independence, however, rests on a different view. It is based on an appeal to "self-evident" truths or "laws of nature and nature's god." The reference to God is vague and subordinated to natural laws that everyone should know through common sense. The Bible is not mentioned or alluded to. The Constitution of 1787 says even less concerning a deity, let alone Christianity or the Bible. The symbolism of the new government was equally secular. In fact, the United States was the first Western nation to omit explicitly Christian symbolism, such as the cross, from its flag and other early national symbols. Further incidental evidence of the founders' own views is the statement from a treaty with the Islamic nation of Tripoli in 1797. This treaty was negotiated under Washington, ratified by the Senate, and signed by President John Adams. The telling part is a description of religion in America: "As the government of the United States of America is not in any sense founded on the Christian Religion,—as it has in itself no character of enmity against the laws, religion or tranquility of Musselmen [i.e., Muslims] . . . , it is declared by the parties that no pretext arising from religious opinions shall ever produce an interruption of the harmony existing between the two countries."[17]

Why does any of this make a difference? Does it really matter if people hold to the mistaken view that America is, or was, or could become a truly Christian nation? Yes, it does matter. It matters because, if we are going to respond effectively to relativistic secularism, then we need to base our response upon reality rather than error. This is not to deny the positive influence that Christianity has indeed had upon the American way of life. Nor is this to minimize the seriousness of secularism. Rather, it is to take it all the more seriously so that we may respond to it all the more effectively.

THE PRACTICAL DILEMMA FOR CHRISTIANS

Was the new republic then just a secular humanist enterprise? If we were to return to the original principles of America's founding documents, would we have to concede the case to today's secularists? Would we have to admit that Christian influences have no place in American public life? Or would we, in order to bring Christianity to bear on national moral life and civil law, actually have to repudiate the founding documents and go back to the Bible as our ultimate constitution and basis for civil law? Would we indeed need a new American revolution?

A Middle Way

The alternatives are not so stark. There is something between the proposals to make the Bible the direct basis for civil law and the militant secularists' vision of eliminating all explicit Christian influence from public life. Despite rhetoric that seems to advocate a Christian theocracy, perhaps this middle way is what some proponents of a return to Christian America have in mind when they mix the ideas of going back to the Bible and back to the founding documents.[18] In any case, the practice of the early republic, to which they sometimes appeal, illustrates such a middle way.

In the early American republic Christian influences were indeed strong,[19] as were some anti-Christian influences. The First Amendment to the Constitution in guaranteeing the free exercise of religion ensured that the federal government would not eliminate Christianity from public life simply because it was a religion. So even established state churches, supported by taxes, continued on in New England into the early nineteenth century. On the other hand, while Christian influences and practices were permitted, the government made no systematic effort to establish explicitly Christian or biblical principles in federal law.

Two points should be emphasized equally here. The first is that, unlike some of the explicit atheism associated with the French Revolution or the Russian Revolution, the American Revolution and the constitutional practice growing out of it were emphatically not anti-Christian or antireligious. Almost everyone in the early republic believed that religion of some sort was good for the nation. The second point is equally important. While religious tolerance left Protestant Christianity in a far more influential position than any other religion, the founding fathers explicitly chose not to make any specific religion the basis for the republic or its policies.

Judged by the political thinking dominant in the Reformation, the American solution was an unacceptable compromise. American government did not guarantee the influence of the Bible on the law of the land. Of course the Bible had been one of the important influences on British law. But in the American nation such influences were haphazard. As Chapter 3 indicated, a whole host of political traditions and ideas of natural law went into the making of Revolutionary thought, and these were decisive in shaping the laws of the land. Such compromises, it might be argued, were both necessary and desirable. But in any case, given this intermingling of influences in shaping early American law, the crucial point is that we should not designate the resultant mixture as simply "biblical," "Judeo-Christian," "Christian," or the like. If we do so, we attribute the authority of God's Word to what is in reality a compromise between biblical and extrabiblical influences.

This blanket endorsement of early America as "biblical," "Judeo-Christian," or "Christian" leads to serious misunderstandings. It attributes to the Bible things that are not drawn from the Bible. Moreover, the idea that a more-or-less generally Christian culture prevailed in America until very recent times lowers the guard of Christians to distinguish what is truly biblical from what is merely part of their cultural heritage.

This argument, so central to the concern of this entire volume, may be worth summarizing:

(1) If it is indeed the case that early America and the early American form of government, while relatively good and influenced by some Christian traditions, were products also of substantial non-Christian influences, and,

(2) if we designate this mixture, without sufficient qualification, as "biblical," "biblically-based," "Judeo-Christian," "Reformation-based," "Christian," or the like,

(3) then (even if we do not intend to) we appear to attribute the authority of God's Word to what is in reality a compromise between biblical and extrabiblical influences.

This conclusion has a practical corollary:

(4) Such confusions, that designate large sections of the American heritage as essentially Christian, have helped to lower the guard of Christians in distinguishing what is truly biblical from what is merely part of their cultural heritage.

Once we get past the dangerous illusion created by attributing the authority of God's Word to the American system of government or way of life, we can nonetheless appreciate the virtues of the early positions of the United States. The American political system is very frankly a system of compromises. We have a system of checks and balances. Regarding religion, no matter how favorable toward Christianity some of the founders may have been, their goal was pluralism, rather than the preferment of one religion to all others. Certainly they did not design the American government so as to ensure that the nation would be Christian in the sense that today Iran is Moslem or Russia is Marxist. Rather the system was intended to guarantee that Christianity and other religions, including various versions of secularized beliefs, *all* should be permitted influence in public discourse. If, as sometimes has happened of late, Christianity is discriminated against simply because it is religious (as in bans of tax support to any explicitly religious school), Christians rightfully should protest within the rules of the system.[20]

What of the place of the Bible, then, as a basis for political action? Should we not bring the nation and its legislation back to the Bible? Here we have to make a careful distinction. Christians' own political decisions should be informed by biblical principles. This is an important point not to miss. Nonetheless, when bringing these decisions to bear on civic debate and legislation we must agree to the rules of the civic game, which under the American constitution are pluralistic. That means that no matter how strongly the Bible or other revelation informs our political views, *for the purposes of civic debate and legislation* we will not appeal simply to religious authority. This is much like the compromise we take for granted as necessary in courts of criminal law. In a murder trial one cannot appeal to a special revelation to provide an exonerating circumstance. In the court, as in much of civic activity, we can leave our Bibles closed and yet find means of expressing biblically informed truths according to rules on which persons of various religions can agree.

Working with Non-Christians: Common Grace

A difficult question yet remains. Is there, any longer, any basis for such constructive political discourse between Christians and non-Christians, particularly on crucial moral questions? The situation today, it is sometimes said, differs from that of the early republic in that then there was a "Christian consensus," or, more accurately, a consensus that included a synthesis of Christian and Enlightenment views of higher moral law. In such a setting Christians and secularists could assume many of the same rules and principles. Today the situation appears very different. Even the definitions of law and truth differ for the Christian and the radical secularist. Law, says the secularist, is determined sociologically and "truth" is relative to time and place. Should we despair, then, of finding a basis for coopera-tion with secularists in public life? Should we declare with Tim LaHaye that "humanists are not qualified to hold public office or to receive taxpayer support for brainwashing their children under the guise of public education?"[21] Must we have it out with the secular humanists to the bitter end in the attempt to establish a government based on the Bible alone?

This choice, so often posed to Christians today, is a false one. We do not live in a world in which all Christians will line up on one side of each public moral issue and all secularists on the other. Many theories today, both those of Christians and of secularists, would seem to predict otherwise. Some Christians speak as though there is an absolute antithesis between Christian and non-Christian thought, neglecting the degree to which Christians themselves are hampered by sin and error, and the degree to which God's common grace allows substantial room for communication and cooperation among all people in practical everyday life. Secularists who accept the radi-cal tenets of relativism make the same mistake. If truth, law, and morality are relative to time, culture, and individual, how can the secularist expect to find any basis for society, since some moral consensus is surely necessary for its survival? In fact, there turns out to be more of a common basis of human beliefs and values than such relativism would suggest. So even Christians and secularists, who may be radically opposed in first principles, often find room for practical agreement and cooperation. Christians are not so consistent in regarding God's law, nor are non-Christians so consistent in disre-garding it for the antithesis between them to be so sharp as we might think.

Christians should not be surprised by this commonality. We are taught, after all, that God's law is written on the hearts of humanity, even if suppressed (Romans 1 and 2). We all live in the same world. God has created laws for living that no one can entirely ignore or escape. Even though it may be plausibly argued that there is no basis for objective knowledge of reality,[22] nonetheless in practical living we all must observe the God-created laws of nature, as when we fly airplanes or pick mushrooms.[23] Similarly, while many of today's thinkers suppose that there is no common base for morality in nature or human nature, in fact no one is entirely free from recognizing the constraints of the moral universe God has created.

Because we all live in God's world, we have, in God's common grace, some basis for discussing and shaping public policy without explicit appeal to the Bible. In fact, people from all the nations of the world have been able to agree on many principles of justice and human interest, as for instance, in agencies and statements of the United Nations. That they violently disagree on other points or on the application of their common principles should not obscure this degree of commonality. So Christians and non-Christians may be able to agree on the value of charity toward the poor and the starving, on the undesirability of genocide, that literacy should be encouraged, on the virtue of loyalty to friends and parents, and on many other things. To be sure, the "light of nature," as America's founding fathers called it, may not be nearly as bright as they supposed. Moreover, there may be, as Augustinians have often argued, a qualitative difference between virtue motivated by love to God and the relatively good that is motivated by other principles.[24] Nonetheless, America's founders were wise in recognizing that the Creator had not left the race so absolutely blind that only those who appealed directly to Scripture were fit to determine public policy.

For Christians, however, the Bible still will play a major role in shaping our approaches to the moral-political issues of the day. Scripture will lead us more directly than will any secular ethical system alone to understanding the principles of God's law. Nonetheless, as we approach these issues we can be sure that if we have correctly identified a biblical principle that should bear upon public policy, that principle will be capable of defense on grounds in addition to the sheer appeal to the authority of Scripture.

Christians will not always persuade fellow citizens "who suppress the truth by their wickedness" (Rom. 1:18). Nonetheless we have in our common experiences with God's created order some basis for discussion. Even on the question of abortion, the most divisive public issue of the day, Christians and non-Christians can agree that the killing of innocent people is wrong. They disagree not so much on the moral principle, but rather on their willingness or unwillingness to admit that abortion is the killing of innocent people. When it comes to nuclear disarmament or gun control, moreover, the sides are often reversed. Secularists will talk of the sanctity of human life, while some Christians, especially politically conservative evangelicals, will speak about the need to defend freedom. These issues will not be easily resolved; but we do have some basis for moral-political discourse without simply bringing the political and legal system "back to the Bible."

The Bible and America's Political Traditions

The counterpart is to realize that "back to the Bible" as the explicit basis for our political life would not be the cure-all we might expect. History illustrates this point abundantly. What could be a more fundamental moral issue than the unprovoked enslavement of one race by another? Ironically, however, Christian influences were crucial to awakening the civilization to this injustice. Yet the more directly the debate was based on the Bible alone, the less possible was a political solution short of a horrible war. When nonslaveholding Christians proclaimed that the Bible demanded immediate emancipation, slaveholding Christians insisted all the more strongly that the Bible sanctioned slavery.[25]

So on many other issues, such as nuclear arms, treatment of the poor, or regulation of the economy, Christians must recognize that the policy implications of the Bible may not be as obvious as we think. The Bible is not a political handbook. Moreover, even though the Bible does not err, its interpreters do. In church life such disagreements and errors are one of the reasons why so many denominations exist. In political life, if every party is certain its position is backed by the sure authority of God, the likelihood of violence increases vastly. Northern Ireland, South Africa, and the entire Middle East should warn us against the dangers of basing politics directly on religious authority.

America's founding fathers wanted to avoid just such possibilities. They knew a lot about "Christian" nations. Most of the European wars of the preceding centuries had some "Christian" motivations. The American founders also knew a lot about Protestant Bible commonwealths; these were a major part of their recent British heritage. So, while the founders appropriated secularized versions of some Puritan ideas about the dangers of monarchy, they purposely chose not to set up a Bible-based republic.

This does not mean that if we want to be consistent with the American constitutional heritage, we must abandon the Bible or the Judeo-Christian tradition in reforming the nation. Cultures and their moral and legal systems are influenced by traditions, usually shaped in part by religious heritages. Even if the American heritage is not "Christian" or biblical in any strict sense, the generically Judeo-Christian aspects of its heritage may be relatively the best available for the health of the civilization. This heritage is inestimably rich in moral wisdom and protects some essential social ideals, such as that the family is a God-ordained structure not to be broken simply because of the will of an individual. Certainly the Judeo-Christian heritage, even mixed as it is with other traditions, is immensely richer than the barren hedonism and relativistic secular philosophies recently contending for social dominance. Christians who are calling in unqualified ways for a return to the Bible are in fact pointing to the legitimate and immensely important cause of preserving the influences of this heritage in opposition to its destructive contemporary rivals. If such a heritage is to be preserved, it will have to be presented as a valuable competitor in the free marketplace of ideas, not as a system that can dictate its own ways on the basis of appeal to the direct authority of God.[26]

We must be careful, moreover, not uncritically to accept generically Christian tradition as a social-political guide. Such tradition is always mixed with other heritages and influences, so we must always test it in the refiner's fire of the biblical witness.

In the social-political arena Christians might argue for the moral superiority of generically Christian traditions. Certainly there seems to be little reason why a moral principle should be placed at a political or legal disadvantage just because it happens to be associated with a traditional religion. Biblical teaching, moreover, should impel Christians to use political means to promote justice and morality, even though in the political arena itself they support these because they are just and moral, not simply because they are biblical or Christian.

None of these qualifications should make us dismiss the genuine issues raised by the advocates of a return to a Christian America. We are in the midst of a cultural crisis. During the past two decades moral relativism has become much more visible in American public life. The constant celebration of self-indulgence that dominates the media and popular culture will certainly take its toll on whatever moral fabric holds a society together. How long, for instance, can the music and entertainment surrounding us dwell on the romance of adultery without adultery being taken for granted? Many of the recent court cases—none more than the approval of abortion-on-demand—reflect a destructive individualistic relativism. Can a society based upon such moral relativism endure for long?

These are crucial issues at stake which every Christian must confront in some way. Such a struggle will involve, first of all, winning hearts and souls to Christian commitment. But beyond this, biblically informed commitment should bring Christians to see the urgency of political action as a God-given means of meeting today's issues concerning morality and justice.

This political side of Christians' action—whether on the political right, left, or middle—should be marked by humility. We should not too readily claim the authority of God for a political or economic program by saying that ours is the "Christian" position. Our motives and our reading of the Bible may seem to us the best; but we should be reminded that the most common use of the Bible in politics has been to justify one's own self-interests. Because we are not immune from this human frailty and because we are imperfect in understanding both the Bible and the dynamics of modern politics, we should think at least twice before claiming to speak with the authority of a Hebrew prophet. We should have Christian approaches to politics, recognizing that there will be a variety of these, but we should not expect to produce "the Christian political program." On a larger scale, given the self-interest and frailty that dominates human behavior, we should not suppose that whole nations are, have been, or in this era will be "Christian" or "biblically based" in the sense of usually following God's will.

Finally, this whole question comes back to what kind of book the Bible is in relation to modern politics. Specifically, which do we emphasize more, the parts of the Old Testament which focus on national Israel, or the themes in both Old and New Testaments which speak to all people? Calvinists in the English Puritan tradition, who have had disproportionately large influence in America, often stressed, as we have seen, nationalistic parts of the Old Testament in assessing our nation. Intimating that America's relationship to God is similar to that of ancient Israel, they long have held up the ideal of "Christian" politics and a "Christian" nation.

If, however, we emphasize more the other side of the American Protestant heritage, that which sees the New Testament as the primary guide to political attitudes in this age, all politics is relativized.

Christians have civic responsibilities and obligations to promote justice. In modern democracies, where to an extent the people rule, these responsibilities are greater than in the Roman Empire. Yet the New Testament nowhere intimates that the Kingdom is political or that it can be identified with a nation or with national objectives. All political solutions, whether the revolutionary dreams of the Zealots or the Roman dreams of a golden age of law and order, take on at best a relative significance in the light of the revelation of Christ, his Kingdom, and the church.

As we pray and work for revival and Christian renewal, we should then reassess the degree to which we should dream of a political reformation or revolution restoring America to her lost "Christian" heritage. Social, political, and moral renewal are proper goals; but to dream of making America a "Christian" nation is at odds not only with the ideals on which the United States was founded—it is also at odds with the deeper message of the whole Bible. For it was the risen Christ himself who explained "the Law of Moses, the Prophets and the Psalms" to his disciples as a message of "repentance and forgiveness of sins . . . to all nations" (Luke 24:44, 47).

RETURN TO CHRISTIAN AMERICA: A POLITICAL AGENDA?: NOTES

[1]In a 1965 sermon, "Ministers and Marchers," Falwell said, "Nowhere are we commissioned to reform the externals." In 1980, he repudiated this sermon as "false prophecy." Frances Fitzgerald, "A Disciplined, Charging Army," *The New Yorker*, May 18, 1981, 63.

[2]From a 1980 statement quoted in Peggy L. Shriver, *The Bible Vote: Religion and the New Right* (New York: The Pilgrim Press, 1981), p. 9.

[3]This summary is a composite from many sources. Some of these are: Jerry Falwell, *Listen, America!* (New York: Doubleday, 1980); Falwell, "Why is America Important to God?" *Journal Champion* 11:8 (Sept. 28, 1979), 1; Falwell, "Why Every American Should Oppose Salt II," *Special Report* (Aug. 1979), 1, 2; Falwell, ed., with Ed Dobson and Ed Hindson, *The Fundamentalist Phenomenon: The Resurgence of Conservative Christianity* (New York: Doubleday, 1980); Tim LaHaye, *The Battle for the Mind* (Old Tappan, NJ: Revell, 1980); Peter Marshall and David Manuel, *The Light and the Glory* (Old Tappan, NJ: Revell, 1977); John R. Price, *America at the Crossroads: Repentance or Repression?* (Indianapolis: Christian House, 1976; cf. Foreword by Dr. Bill Bright); James Robison with Jim Cox, *Save America to Save the World* (Wheaton, IL: Tyndale, 1980); Jack Van Impe, "Can America Survive?" An Independence Day Message (Royal Oaks, MI: Jack Van Impe Crusades, 1976); Van Impe, "America, We Love You!" *Perhaps Today:* III:2 (July/Aug. 1982), 1-7, 30.

⁴*Op. cit., Listen, America,* p. 50.

⁵*Op. cit., Battle for the Mind,* p. 36.

⁶For examples, Harry Conn, *Four Trojan Horses of Humanism* (Milford, MI: Mott Media, 1982 [1978]); John W. Whitehead, *The Second American Revolution* (Elgin, IL: David C. Cook, 1982); and works by Falwell and LaHaye, above.

⁷Cf. Henry May, *The Enlightenment in America* (New York: Oxford), pp. 59-64, 337-350; and George M. Marsden, *Fundamentalism and American Culture: The Shaping of Twentieth-Century Evangelicalism* (New York: Oxford, 1980), pp. 37, 99-101, and elsewhere.

⁸For example, see Richard M. DeVos with Charles Paul Conn, *Believe!* (Old Tappan, NJ: Revell, 1975). DeVos has been a major financial supporter of political campaigns against secular humanism.

⁹E.g., James Robison, "Secular Humanism," tape of TV sermon (1980) says that only recently did he look into the subject of the threat of secular humanism.

¹⁰Although this is an oversimplification, this view does seem to be the general position of Jerry Falwell, Tim LaHaye, Peter Marshall and David Manuel, Jack Van Impe and others (cf. Note 3 above). For an earlier statement of a similar view, cf. Rousas J. Rushdoony, *This Independent Republic: Studies in the Nature and Meaning of American History* (Nutley, NJ: Craig Press, 1964). The views of Francis A. Schaeffer, often appropriated by advocates of a return to a Christian America, are better qualified. Schaeffer emphasizes that the founding of the United States was directly influenced by a prevailing "Christian consensus" and by Reformation ideas. These have been replaced by secular humanism. But Schaeffer does not call directly for a return to Reformation political conditions or to a "biblical America" or a "Christian America." He emphasizes that "we are in no way talking about any kind of theocracy" or "a linking of church and state." "We must not confuse the Kingdom of God with our country. To say it another way: We should not wrap Christianity in our national flag" (*A Christian Manifesto,* Westchester, IL: Crossway Books, 1981), pp. 120 and 121. Schaeffer's political proposals stress restoring the "liberty and justice for all" guaranteed in the founding documents. Religious freedom, he argues, has been unduly restricted and the liberty intended in the First Amendment should be restored. "With this freedom Reformation Christianity would compete in the free marketplace of ideas" (pp. 135-137). However, apparently because of the overwhelming importance he sees in the abortion issue, Schaeffer has associated himself closely with those (e.g., the Moral Majority) who often have not been careful to distinguish between efforts to guard religious liberty and suggestions that specifically Judeo-Christian beliefs and practices be given privileged positions in American law and education (e.g., requiring public schools to teach the creation-science movement's arguments that attempt to authenticate scientifically a literal interpretation of Genesis 1). (Cf. *A Christian Manifesto,* pp. 109-110, which, however, mistakes this for a religious liberty issue.) Schaeffer also has endorsed the work of John W. Whitehead, *The Second American Revolution* (Elgin, IL: David C. Cook, 1982), who repudiates the current concept of pluralism which says "that a Christian should not seek to force his or her religious beliefs on another" (p. 164). Cf. his view on the Bible as the only proper basis for civil law (Note 16 below). To add to the confusion, Schaeffer's son and close associate, Franky Schaeffer, seems to hold a Christian nation ideal when he says, "We must reestablish the beauty and fullness in love of a Christian nation that was once ours" (*A Time for*

Anger: The Myth of Neutrality, Westchester, IL: Crossway, 1982, p. 78). A more critical assessment of the elder Schaeffer's views on these points is provided by Ronald A. Wells in "Francis Schaeffer's Jeremiad: A Review Article," *The Reformed Journal* 32:5 (May 1982), 16-20, and "Whatever Happened to Francis Schaeffer?" *The Reformed Journal* 33:5 (May 1983), 10-13.

[11]See Chapter 2.

[12]Francis Schaeffer attempts to make this link by reference to the Scottish Presbyterian Samuel Rutherford and his volume *Lex Rex or the Law and the Prince* (1644). Writing at the time of the English Puritan revolution, Rutherford argued that God's higher law stood above kings and princes. Since the Declaration of Independence appeals to the authority of "the laws of nature and of nature's god," Schaeffer argues that the Declaration is reflective of the Reformation world view enunciated by Samuel Rutherford. Schaeffer is right that the idea of a higher law standing above magistrates was indeed widespread in the colonies, as it was also in western Europe during the eighteenth century. The idea, however, did not come to the colonies from Rutherford, who does not appear to be especially well known in the American colonies. None of his works were ever republished in America during the colonial period. (Cf. Clifford K. Shipton and James E. Mooney, *National Index of American Imprints Through 1800* [Worcester, MA: American Antiquarian Society and Barre, 1969].) Even John Witherspoon, the Scottish-American clergyman revolutionary, seems not to have referred to Rutherford. (Cf. the four-volume edition of *Witherspoon's Works* published in Philadelphia in 1802, by William W. Woodward; note especially that Rutherford is not referred to in Witherspoon's thirty-two authorities cited at the end of his lectures on ethics and politics; *Works,* III, pp. 471, 472.) Although the idea of a higher law did find expression in the Declaration of Independence, it cannot be linked specifically to Rutherford and in turn to Witherspoon. The idea was held widely in Europe and the colonies, by both Christians and by secularists such as Thomas Paine who violently attacked the Bible. Schaeffer is correct, however, in stating that the idea of a higher law has been largely replaced in recent decades by what he calls "sociological law," or a thoroughgoing secular relativism. Cf. John W. Whitehead, *The Second American Revolution* (Elgin, IL: Cook, 1982), who follows Schaeffer on this point. An interesting dissent is offered by C. Gregg Singer, *A Theological Interpretation of American History* (Philadelphia: Presbyterian and Reformed, 1964), who argues that the Declaration had an "essentially anti-Christian character," p. 40. Singer sees, however, a resurgence of Calvinistic influences in shaping the Constitution in 1787.

[13]It should be noted that this weakened view of the Fall and highly optimistic view of human nature is the same kind of error which Schaeffer attributes to Thomas Aquinas and Erasmus. (Cf. the discussion in Chapter 4 on Witherspoon; and Schaeffer, *How Should We Then Live?*, pp. 51, 52 and 82-84.) Following Schaeffer's own line of argument we would conclude that the extent to which the founding documents were grounded in *nature* rather than *grace,* as was largely the case in the thinking of the founding fathers, meant secularism was given a foothold right from the beginning of the country.

[14]Although Schaeffer does not in fact advocate the Christian America point of view, he seems to conflate the Reformation era with the eighteenth century. The height of the Reformation era came two centuries before the founding of the United

States. Probably the world changed as much or more from 1576 to 1776 as it did from 1776 to 1976. The scientific revolution transformed the Western world from an essentially medieval civilization to a modern one. In 1576 people looked to authorities from the past when they sought truth. In 1776 they more often looked to themselves. One of the things to change most concerns the relation of the Bible and Christianity to politics. During the Reformation era Protestants and Catholics alike assumed that their nations should be explicitly Christian; the state would support the true church and banish or penalize other denominations or religions. One of the significant contributions of the United States Constitution was to *depart* from the Reformation views by rejecting the political establishment of any particular religion. Few would advocate the political establishment of religion in America today. Thus we must recognize that we cannot uncritically or in a wholesale manner appropriate Reformation political views and apply them directly to our own era.

[15]An extreme version of this view is represented by the "theonomy" movement made up of Calvinists who propose to base modern legal systems on Old Testament law. See, for instance, Greg L. Bahnsen, *Theonomy in Christian Ethics* (Nutley, NJ: Craig Press, 1979).

[16]See further, *op. cit.*, *The Second American Revolution*, p. 73, where Whitehead writes: "Law in the true sense is bibliocentric, concerned with justice in terms of the Creator's revelation." This means, Whitehead says, that there is no legitimate natural-law basis for civil law apart from reference to the Bible. Pp. 73-82, 181-192.

[17]Harold O. J. Brown, *The Reconstruction of the Republic* (Milford, MI: Mott Media, 1981 [1977]), p. 35, discusses the symbols. For a copy of the treaty, see Hunter Miller, *Treaties and Other International Acts of the United States* (Washington: Government Printing Office, 1930), II, p. 365.

[18]*Op. cit.*, Harold O. J. Brown, *The Reconstruction of the Republic*, avoids this confusion while calling for a return to Christian traditions. Some statements of Francis Schaeffer might be read as advocating a more thoroughgoing pluralism than the call for a return to Reformation principles would suggest.

[19]Virtually every recent study of the ideological origins of the American Revolution has pointed out the pervasive influence of generically Christian political traditions. The extent and some of the limits of such influences in the early republic are indicated in Fred J. Hood, *Reformed America: The Middle and Southern States, 1783-1837* (University, Ala.: University of Alabama Press, 1980).

[20]Cf. Rockne McCarthy and James Skillen, *Disestablishment a Second Time: Genuine Pluralism for American Schools* (Grand Rapids: Eerdmans, 1982).

[21]*Op. cit.*, *Battle for the Mind*, p. 36.

[22]Most famously in Thomas S. Kuhn, *The Structure of Scientific Revolutions* (Chicago: University of Chicago Press, 1962).

[23]Francis Schaeffer has made this point most effectively in pointing out the impossibility of living consistently with relativistic secularist world views—e.g. *The God Who Is There* (1968); *The Complete Works of Francis A. Schaeffer: A Christian Worldview* (Westchester, IL: Crossway Books, 1982), Vol. I, pp. 137, 138.

[24]This sort of distinction is precisely the kind made by America's greatest evangelical theologian, Jonathan Edwards, in his discussion of *The Nature of True Virtue* (originally published 1765, available in a paperback edited by William K.

Frankena, Ann Arbor: University of Michigan Press, 1960). Edwards conceded that people, by nature, do many useful and valuable deeds, but he argued that these are done from self-interest or self-love unless the individual has been changed by God's grace. *True* virtue, he contended, describes a person only when we do our useful and socially valuable deeds for the glory of our Creator and Redeemer.

[25]On the biblical defense of slavery, see Donald G. Mathews, *Religion in the Old South* (Chicago: University of Chicago Press, 1977), pp. 152, 157, 158, 175, 176; Anne C. Loveland, *Southern Evangelicals and the Social Order, 1800-1860* (Baton Rouge: Louisiana State University Press, 1980), pp. 194, 199-203; and David Brion Davis, *The Problem of Slavery in the Age of Revolution* (Ithaca, NY: Cornell University Press, 1975), pp. 523-556.

[26]See Note 18 above.

CHAPTER SEVEN

"The Clean Sea-breeze of the Centuries": Learning to Think Historically

By a triple birthright American evangelicals bring a healthy skepticism to the past—even to our own history. As children of the Reformation, we cling to Scripture rather than tradition as authoritative. As Americans, citizens of "the first new nation,"[1] we dislike granting one generation authority over another, and we cherish commitments that we make ourselves rather than those handed down to us. We are prone to dismiss conventional wisdom and hidebound systems. As heirs of fundamentalism, finally, we bristle at the suggestion that the natural historical process, rather than the supernatural, governs the course of events. Such a legacy has made it difficult for evangelicals to bring the past into focus, and difficult as well to use the past to gain a truer image of ourselves. Whatever our strengths in seizing the moment in God's name, we evangelicals are inexperienced in practicing fellowship with Christians across the centuries. But since we do not practice this kind of fellowship, we lose a great privilege—nothing less than discovering where we ourselves, and our ideas and prejudices, stand in the stream of the centuries. To use an image of C. S. Lewis, we need practice in opening windows to "the clean sea-breeze of the centuries."[2]

This entire book has assumed that it is a valuable thing to avail ourselves of the experience of Christians in the past. But why? Can we spell it out clearly here? The first thing to say is that throughout redemptive history, God himself has appealed to his people on the basis of his history with them. This is true in the Old Testament most noticeably in the mighty act of the Exodus, the "Magna Charta" of the children of Israel (Deuteronomy 6:20-23; 26:5-10). The eminent Christian historian Herbert Butterfield has even suggested that, more than anything else, it was the power of its historical memory that held Israel together as a people.[3] In the New Testament, Hebrews 11 similarly counsels us to heed those who, though dead, still are speaking (11:4). Surrounded by such a cloud of witnesses (12:1), we become empowered to run with perseverance the race set before us.

On a personal level such fellowship across generations can serve to inspire, warn, instruct, and broaden. God, to be sure, can give such gifts in any number of ways—natural and supernatural. But he normally uses human agents to stir up his people. For those whose Christian walk has become mediocre plodding, there is no source of inspiration better than an encounter with Bernard of Clairvaux, St. Francis, or John Wycliffe from the Middle Ages; with Martin Luther, John Wesley, Menno Simons, or the other Protestant founders; with the Countess of Huntingdon who inspired both revival and social reform in the eighteenth century; with missionary pioneers like Adoniram Judson; or with those whose faith overcame great barriers like Richard Allen, founder of the African Methodist Episcopal Church. Just as the past can deliver us from smallness of vision, so can it also caution against error, excess, and failure. How foolish to think that we cannot learn vivid lessons from the mistakes of those who have already run the course.

By its instruction, history can also deliver us from the tyranny of our own times, the conceit that we are necessarily wiser than our forebears—what C. S. Lewis called chronological snobbery. Through reading Christian classics we can sit at the feet of John of the Cross to learn about prayer, Martin Luther about grace, John Calvin about faith, Jonathan Edwards about revivals. And we can hear the message of the poets—Charles Wesley on the new creation, William Cowper on depression, and Count Zinzendorf on the blood of Christ. Exploring the length and breadth of historic Christendom can also broaden our thinking in the best sense. It removes the blinkers of our own limited backgrounds—whether Arminian, Calvinist, fundamentalist, Catholic, Lutheran, Church of Christ, Pentecostal, or whatever—and opens us to the riches of God's work in other traditions.

Yet beyond these benefits, there is an even more compelling reason to acquire an intimate knowledge of the past. When we gain such an acquaintance, we can begin to comprehend the characteristic assumptions of our own age, particularly its blindnesses, those unexamined habits of mind about which future generations will ask, "But how *could* they have thought that?" C. S. Lewis advocated the reading of old books as "the clean sea-breeze of the centuries," precisely for this reason. Only the past, he said, could provide steady coordinates to orient the Christian in the contemporary world:

> Not that the past has any magic about it, but because we cannot study the future, and yet need something to set against the present, to remind us that the basic assumptions have been quite different in different periods and that much which seems certain to the uneducated is merely temporary fashion. A man who has lived in many places is not likely to be deceived by the local errors of his native village; the scholar has lived in many times and is therefore in some degree immune for the great cataract of nonsense that pours from the press and the microphone of his own age.[4]

Christians are never immune from the cultural values of their age and are always in danger of equating Christianity with contemporary ideals. But history, by analyzing the sources of such values and assumptions, can identify some of the formative cultural elements that have either shaped or distorted our understanding of God and his revelation. We can thereby begin to differentiate between what is normative and what is time-bound. In exploring the untested assumptions that shape us, the role of the historian is like that of the psychologist:

> In somewhat the same way that unconscious and subconscious factors influence our psychological development, deep-seated cultural patterns, ideals, values, and assumptions exert a subtle and often unrecognized influence on everyone in that culture. To the extent that these influences remain unconscious we are controlled by them; but to the extent that we are made conscious of these influences we are in a position to discriminate among them and to exercise a degree of control over them. So, as the analyst brings unconscious psychological factors into consciousness by tracing their roots back to their childhood origins, the historian brings cultural patterns, ideals, values and assumptions to consciousness by tracing them back to their historical origins. If only the present is considered, current political and social patterns, as well as general cultural ideals, often appear to have a certain inevitability about them. Once it is seen, however, how these patterns or ideals developed, who first formulated them, what preceded them, and what were the alternatives, they lose that illusion of inevitability and it is possible not only to understand them better but also to discriminate among them according to Christian principles.[5]

The benefits of Christian history are clear enough: an immediate relevance for clarifying both the gospel and the taken-for-granted assumptions of the contemporary world. Yet learning to think historically is neither simple nor self-evident, particularly for those who—like many evangelicals—become enthusiastic about its promise but are unskilled in discerning its lessons. The chief obstacle is the assumption that opening windows to the past is a snap, as simple as turning a latch; whereas, in fact, it is a delicate procedure which in haste many have abused.

The simplest and most appealing way to think about the past, in fact, is the most dangerous. It is to survey the historical landscape with a preference for that which is similar to or that which anticipates the present. Thus the ecumenist, when coming to history, finds its direction and movement in ecumenical successes, the high-church devotee in the church's organic development, the pacifist in peace movements, the fundamentalist in militant defenses of the truth, the social activist in examples of reform. Once we begin with our own commitments, the selection of the facts to fit them is all too easy, the more so since selectivity is usually unconscious. The parts of the story which we underline are very often merely just the ones that seem important because they bear out our own convictions. Yet such a search for similarity in the past ironically actually saps history of its relevance: the past becomes little more than a screen upon which we project our own concerns. Rather than offering genuine insight into our own times, the past becomes just one more medium to convey positions which we already hold. To approach history this way is tragic, for it means that we lose the ability really to learn from the past. Yet it is also very common and may in fact be done in a variety of forms, four of which deserve mention.

THE PAST AS MIRROR

Some of us are so zealous about our own commitments that the past does nothing but mirror back our own preconceptions. We readily study the past, and often become enthralled in it. But by a subtle and often unconscious process we pick out of the historical tapestry only those strands which reinforce our own points of view. This selective use of history is rife on both sides of such contemporary debates as the nature of Christian political responsibility, the inerrancy of the Bible, and the role of women in the church. Apart from any of the specific issues at stake, the tragedy is that we come to believe that we are attuned to the wisdom of the ages when in fact the sound we really hear is but an echo of our own voice. The past thus offers no critical perspective on our own times at the exact moment when we think we have become its devoted pupils.

THE PAST AS ESCAPE

A quest to recover history can also be misplaced if it does not begin by coming to terms with one's own history. Christians who do not have a strong sense of history often overreact when first they catch the allure of the past. It is then easy to overshoot the mark when trying to recover the historic riches of the church. In our own day, for instance, it is easy enough to understand the surprising number who have shed an informal, low church heritage—often, in America, a tradition without tradition—for the historic continuities found in the Episcopal or Catholic churches. In an extreme example, one group which came out of the "Jesus Movement" of the 1960s has now swung so far in the direction of reverencing tradition that it has formed a new "Orthodox" church which seeks relations with the Eastern branches of Christendom, supposedly the purest strains of early Christian tradition.

What is more perplexing is that so often this impulse to find continuity begins by a decisive and unthinking break from one's own history and tradition. A double irony is involved when people claim to exalt history on the one hand, and have no respect for their own tradition on the other. In the first place, it is patently ahistorical to assume that one can, by sheer act of will, rend those ties which Providence has allowed naturally to grow, attempting instead to graft one's soul onto stock that appears more acceptable. The action of not taking seriously the work of God in one's own tradition and in one's own personal development speaks much louder than a river of words about the importance of returning to Christian roots. The second irony is that those who attempt to escape their own history generally do not understand it, and thus will likely be shaped by it long after asserting their independence.

THE PAST AS GOLDEN AGE

A third misuse of history is the call for Christians today to emulate the virtues of some bygone era—the Early Church Fathers, the world of St. Thomas in the thirteenth century, the period of the Reformation, the Puritan era, the age of Wesley, or the Early American Republic. Christians should walk up and down the breadth of historic Christianity, to be sure. But they run great risk in holding up any one given age as a model or a panacea for contemporary ills.

This search for a historic golden age generally involves a false comparison: lining up the best of a past period or movement against the stark reality of the present, with all its failure, inconsistency, and hypocrisy. This is a common tendency whenever Christians become troubled about their own times. They are then naturally prone to look for ways to shore up virtues that seem to be slipping away. By searching out evidence in the historical record, they hope to stabilize the present with firm historical moorings.

This tendency often leads us to contrast our own secular and permissive age, for instance, with an idyllic picture of the Early American Republic as a Christian nation. There is, however, a threefold problem in depicting such a standard from which we are said to have fallen. Often, to be sure, the specific claims about the earlier period may be true—in this case, that early America was generally Christian in the structure of its law, its institutions, and its culture. Yet the fallacy lies in what remains unsaid, in the failure to recognize how profoundly different the world of the late eighteenth and early nineteenth century was from our own, and in the method by which such an image of the past is constructed. In the first place, the approach is extremely selective. It fails to take into account some of the countervailing evidence that we have seen in earlier chapters: the 80 to 85 percent of Americans who at the time of the Revolution were not church members, the success of un-Christian currents of thought in beguiling the generation of the founding fathers, the institution of slavery that Christians allowed to be legitimated in the Constitution, and the testimony of Christians from that generation who were painfully aware of the rampant ungodliness in their society and the paltry influence of Christian thinking in their politics.

If the first mistake is presenting a half-truth, the second is wrenching events and ideas from their original context. To depict early America as a Christian nation, without further clarification, leaves the impression that the only difference of consequence between that age and our own is between strong faith and weak, genuine courage and feigned, serious thinking and shallow, noble purpose and selfish. Assuming the similarity of past and present, this vision overlooks the profound Christian legacy that Western society enjoyed in the early modern period—capital for which individuals in that day were not themselves responsible and which we today find largely spent. It also ignores major elements of change. In the infant republic nine out of ten citizens (i.e., white males) could claim a heritage that was British and Protestant. The radical pluralism—of ethnic origin, religion, and culture—that has developed in the two centuries since the Revolution places almost every public decision today about religion or morality in a different context. Whatever positions Christians may take in responding to a secular world, working to turn back the clock—as if nothing had changed in the meantime—is the surest means of failing to meet those challenges which are uniquely today's.

The third fallacy of depicting such a golden age of Christian influence concerns the method by which we reconstruct the past. The danger is simply that we project an image of our forebears that combines the happy solution of our own difficulties and the realization of our own deepest longings. In doing so, we are not only incorrect with respect to the historical record, but also counterproductive in helping our own age. Rather than stirring people to action, a falsely idealistic view of the past leaves a bitter residue—the conviction that God, who moved mightily among his people in ages past, is strangely silent amidst our own trouble and perplexities.

THE PAST AS ORDERLY CHAIN OF CAUSE AND EFFECT

Christians are taught that the basic issues of life are simple: to trust as a child, to speak with a simple yes or no, to love unfeigned, to maintain undivided loyalties. All of this presupposes that God has made plain to us the difference between truth and error, light and darkness, and that he ordained the goal to which certain kinds of thought and behavior predictably lead. It seems reasonable, therefore, that the record of human history, if intelligible at all, would mirror divine morality in such a way as to enable us to see clearly the right and the wrong and to chart precisely the triumph of good and the disastrous consequences of evil. History, in this view, is something that clarifies the difference between the broad road and the straight and narrow; it serves as a beam of unrefracted light illuminating the meaning and purpose of life.

Yet the more we actually examine the way things have happened, the more we are driven from the simple to the complex. This is the central dilemma for anyone coming to study the past, as Herbert Butterfield suggests in his work *The Whig Interpretation of History.* The problem becomes even more exaggerated for the Christian who expects history to echo in unmistakable tones the manifest purposes of God as revealed in Scripture. "The truth of history," Butterfield wrote, "is no simple matter, all packed and parcelled ready for handling in the market place." History is not unrefracted light, confirming the ultimate validity of ideals themselves, but light as it breaks up into color in the external world, introducing us to the role of ideals in the lives of fallible women and men. The historian is not free to speculate with the theologian or philosopher on what might or should have happened; he must faithfully observe principles "caught amongst chance and accident; he must watch their logic being tricked and entangled in the events of a concrete world."[6]

The natural response to such complexity is to simplify the historical process in order to reclaim for history a more certain voice. Christians in particular are prone to abbreviate the historical record, pruning from the past that which is messy in order to enjoy clear illustrations of true and false teaching, avoiding the complex in order to find inspiring examples of godly and ungodly living. We do this less by a conscious principle of exclusion and more by the initial assumption that the past speaks only in such affirmative tones. Yet for all its clarity and illustrative power, such "history" is an optical illusion that distorts the past and compromises the truth.

The real mistake is in overdramatizing the historical process, imputing historical change to some direct agency, and patching all evidence into a neat story that vindicates those priorities which we hold dear, which seem to us self-evident. We forget that the unfolding of history rarely affords front-row seats for observing the clash of antithetical world views. More often, what we see in the real world of individuals and groups is a mingling of truth and error. We behold vivid strengths coupled with vivid weaknesses. We find opposing points of view both of which seem to grasp truth in part but not in full. We discover people unaware of what really controls their thinking. We come across admirable goals which end in disastrous out-workings, evil intentions that eventuate in good, and positive out-comes that no one at first seemed to desire.

The time of the American Revolution, as earlier chapters have shown, offers just such a situation. No clearly defined contest ex-isted between Christian and Enlightenment thinkers to see who would serve as the architects of the American republic. For all the Christian values resonant in that culture, the thinking of men such as James Madison or John Witherspoon can at best be described as a patchwork of Enlightenment and Christian ideas. They were sur-prisingly unselfconscious, furthermore, about the sources of their ideas or the ends to which they pointed. Equally ambiguous was American Christianity in the years before the Civil War. That period offers us contrasting solutions to moral and national problems, both of which seem valid but incomplete: zealous social activists, like the abolitionists Arthur and Lewis Tappan, who cared not a whit about sound theology; and zealous defenders of the faith, such as Charles Hodge at Princeton, who with the best theological arguments kept pressing social issues at arm's length.[7]

A similar error is the assumption that we have the capacity to trace all historical events back to their primary human agents. If we think we can always discern the connections between personal causes and large-scale social effects, we are in grave danger of telescoping the complexity of interactions that make up the historical process into a simple progression. And we are in danger of believing that we can invariably tell how specific individuals with particular intentions were the exact causes of certain events. But history usually reveals no simple link between cause and effect, intention and outcome. The complications of human affairs are often too great for our capacities; they regularly cheat us of their purposes and deflect their labors to unpredictable ends—at least to human wisdom. The rise of religious liberty, Butterfield suggests, was not the logical outworking of either Protestantism or Catholicism, but actually of the prolonged clash between them and the resulting rise of religious indifference. Out of this clash of will, something emerged which neither side had sought. In a similar irony, the American Revolution became imbued with a religious cast not because Christians of that era were especially adept at applying Christianity to politics, but because so many people of religious fervor came to consider the political order of as much ultimate concern as the church itself. The same kind of intensity that Jonathan Edwards used in proclaiming the need for repentance and faith, John and Samuel Adams displayed in declaring the need for political liberty. In this sense the American Revolution represents more the product of a residual Christianity, its base deeply eroded, than it does the infusion of genuine Christian principles into politics.

Christians, of all people, should not be surprised that the historical process is deeply ironic. Redemptive history, after all, is one story after another of God turning the intentions of men, good and bad, to his own better and wiser purpose. Joseph's brothers intended to kill him, but God deflected this evil to the rescue of an entire people. "You intended to harm me; but God intended it for good" (Genesis 50:30). From the monarchy, which Israel had erected in defiance, God raised up the house of David in whose seed all nations would be blessed. In history's ultimate irony death and hell were crushed at the cross even as they exulted in momentary triumph.

The complexity and irony of history blast all our cherished notions and our pet theories. But they do convey to the Christian a strong word of consolation. History, fortunately, is subject neither to the designs of evil men nor the frailty and foibles of good ones. While the past does provide an ample measure of vision, direction, warning and inspiration, its complexity forces us, in the final analysis, to admit that the process defies our limited comprehension. We must analyze the past as carefully as we can. And we must continue to act in the present on the basis of our best analyses of the past. But we should never be overconfident or presumptuous. We should never think that we have mastered history. "It would not be strange," noted C. S. Lewis, "if we, who have not sat through the whole play, and who have heard only tiny fragments of the scenes already played, sometimes mistook a mere [extra] in a fine dress for one of the protagonists."[8] Amidst the complexity of the historical record, a "labyrinthine network" in Butterfield's words, we are left with nothing historical in which to trust—nothing save the mighty arm of God which, by breaking into history, closed the yawning gates of hell and turns even the clenched fist of man's wrath to his praise.

In the last analysis, this is the attitude which we must carry with us as we face the crises of our day. No easy solutions from the past are going to resolve the profound questions which surround us—of life and death, truth and morality, peace and justice. At the same time, we may not hide behind the complexities, ambiguities, and uncertainties of history as an excuse for inaction. Although history provides no magical key to truth and morality, Christians still must labor without ceasing for truth and morality in the midst of our own age. This is a task to which every Christian is called; and it is a task which bears upon the full range of human life—in business, academics, the home, politics, evangelism, law. In each area Christians must enter into the struggle, using the means which are appropriate within each area of calling. The purpose of this book is to help us be more effective in that struggle, especially by allowing a more realistic view of history to disperse our foggy notions of the past and to clarify our perceptions of the present.

"THE CLEAN SEA-BREEZE OF THE CENTURIES": NOTES

[1]Seymour M. Lipset, *The First New Nation: The United States in Historical and Comparative Perspective* (New York: Basic Books, 1963).

[2]C. S. Lewis, "On the Reading of Old Books," in *God in the Dock: Essays on Theology and Ethics* (Grand Rapids: Eerdmans, 1970), p. 202.

[3]Herbert Butterfield, *The Origins of History* (New York: Basic Books, 1981), pp. 80-117.

[4]C. S. Lewis, "Learning in War-Time," in *The Weight of Glory and Other Essays* (New York: Macmillan, 1980), pp. 28, 29.

[5]George M. Marsden, "A Christian Perspective for the Teaching of History," in *A Christian View of History?*, Marsden and Frank Roberts, eds. (Grand Rapids: Eerdmans, 1975), p. 44.

[6]Herbert Butterfield, *The Whig Interpretation of History* (London: G. Bell, 1931), pp. 66, 67.

[7]See Bertram Wyatt-Brown, *Lewis Tappan and the Evangelical War Against Slavery* (Cleveland: Case Western, 1969); and William S. Barker, "The Social View of Charles Hodge (1797-1878): A Study in Nineteenth-Century Calvinism and Conservatism," *Presbyterion: Covenant Seminary Review*, 1 (Spring 1975), 1-22.

[8]C. S. Lewis, "Historicism," in *Christian Reflections* (Grand Rapids: Eerdmans, 1967), p. 110.

APPENDIX

The Search for Christian America: A Bibliographical Essay

by Randall H. Balmer

When Alexis de Tocqueville made his famous tour of nineteenth-century America, he wrote: "On my arrival in the United States the religious aspect of the country was the first thing that struck my attention." The French observer was neither the first nor the last to detect a unique relationship between the American character and religion; even so enlightened a figure as Benjamin Franklin proposed that the seal of the new nation depict Moses leading the children of Israel across the Red Sea.

Much literature has been written on this relationship. Some writers argue strongly for its existence. Others take the religious character of America for granted and attempt to use it for one purpose or another. Still others conclude that the connection has had both positive and negative results. And the historical research of another group of scholars calls into question whether or not America truly was ever Christian in any but a nominal sense. This essay explores selective examples of these kinds of literature, from both the past and the present. It begins with those writers—historical and contemporary—who emphasize a strong relationship between Christianity and the founding of this nation. The essay then discusses some of the scholarly works which have explored the ramifications of this perception. A third section suggests some studies of general historical themes which provide information for those who wish to discover for themselves to what extent Christianity has been a decisive influence. And it concludes by offering a brief discussion of works which employ a realistic picture of America's heritage to chart Christian action in our own day. For each of the works mentioned in this essay a full title and date of publication are found at the end of the chapter.

THE BELIEF IN CHRISTIAN AMERICA

When Thomas Prince sat down early in the eighteenth century to write a history of New England, he began his account with creation. So convinced was he that America occupied a special place in God's design that all of divine and human history since Genesis served as prelude to the Puritan migration from England to America in the 1630s.

Prince never completed his history, but his belief that America occupied a vaunted place in God's Kingdom has not been unusual. Both before Prince's day and after, a goodly number of Americans have eagerly pointed out this land's divine connections. Alexander Whitaker was one of the first. His *Good Newes from Virginia* noted the "almost miraculous beginning, and continuance of this plantation" and added that "God hath opened this passage unto us, and led us by the hand unto this work." William Bradford's chronicle *Of Plymouth Plantation* credited the success of the Pilgrim venture in the New World to "the special work and hand of God." Crossing the Atlantic aboard the *Arbella* in 1630, John Winthrop invoked biblical images to describe the Puritans' mission to the New World. His sermon "A Modell of Christian Charity" expressed confidence that "the God of Israell is among us," that New England "shall be as a Citty upon a Hill," and that "the Lord our God may blesse us in the land whither we go to possesse it." Similarly, Edward Johnson's *Wonder-Working Providence of Sions Saviour in New England* contrasted God's chosen people of New England with the "irreligious lascivious and popish affected persons" they left behind in England. And Cotton Mather opened *Magnalia Christi Americana* saying, "It hath been deservedly esteemed, one of the great and wonderful Works of God in this *Last Age,* that the Lord stirred up the Spirits of so many Thousands of his Servants, to leave the *Pleasant Land of England.*"

During times of crisis in America's past its leaders have summoned the theme of chosenness with special intensity; stories of this land's uniqueness in God's eyes thereby serve as an impetus for spiritual and cultural revitalization. The self-appointed guardians of New England's spiritual health discerned a subtle decline in religious fervor shortly after 1650. Accordingly, various Puritan ministers sounded the alarm, calling their congregations back to the piety of the colony's founders. In 1662, the "time of the great drought" and the year that standards for church membership were relaxed (which many believed to be a sure sign of spiritual declension), Michael Wigglesworth wrote *God's Controversy with New England.* Wigglesworth recalled the divine origins of the colony's settlement ("The glorious Lord of hostes / Was pleased to lead his armies forth / Into those forrein coastes") and entreated the Puritans to live up to their spiritual heritage or face even "sorer judgements" from an angry God.

Ministers such as Nicholas Noyes believed that leaders in the colonies, the King's magistrates, had a special obligation to God's chosen people in the New World. In *New-Englands Duty and Interest* he wrote: "This People of *New England* are a People whom God hath Signally owned & blessed." Magistrates had an obligation, then, to see that New England became a "Habitation of Justice, and Mountain of Holiness." Throughout its history many have even felt that this land would play a central role in ushering in the Millennium. Stirred by the miraculous workings of the Great Awakening, no less a figure than Jonathan Edwards published his chiliastic hopes in an essay called "The Latter-Day Glory is Probably to Begin in America."

America's notion of uniqueness, however, has frequently led to effects less benign than the Millennium's ideal of a thousand-year peace. When the French—whom many colonists considered to be godless papists—loomed as a military threat on the frontier in the early eighteenth century, ministers and others began to use the language of chosenness to marshal troops for battle or to celebrate military victories. Samuel Niles's *Brief and Plain Essay,* for example, exulted in the defeat of the heretical French by "godly Soldiers" committed to "the cause of God." Similarly, the Reverend Samuel Davies of Virginia preached sermons entitled *Religion and Patriotism, the Constituents of a Good Soldier* and *The Curse of Cowardice* to rally the recruits for the French and Indian War. Samuel Checkley joined the chorus with a sermon entitled *The Duty of God's People when Engaged in War,* assuring his auditors that "GOD will be on their Side" and that they "may comfort themselves with this Thought that they are fighting *the Lord's Battles.*" John Lowell, meanwhile, was convinced of *The Advantages of God's Presence with his People in an Expedition against their Enemies.*

The militant rhetoric surrounding the French and Indian War laid the foundation for the Revolution itself. In a 1777 sermon entitled *God Arising and Pleading His People's Cause,* Abraham Keteltas concluded that "the cause of this American Continent, against the masures [*sic*] of a cruel, bloody, and vindictive ministry [the English government], is the cause of God." In *The Church's Flight into the Wilderness,* a sermon dedicated to John Hancock, Samuel Sherwood declared that God "has, of his unmerited grace, bestowed liberties and privileges upon [America], beyond what are enjoyed in any other part of the world." Cyprian Strong was confident that his text, the fifth chapter of Isaiah, was "strictly applicable to the church and people of this land; or this American vineyard." After frequent allusions to the piety of New England's founders, Strong warned that, like ancient Israel, "we have great reason to fear that God will withdraw his favorable presence from us" unless his chosen people show "deep repentance, humiliation and reformation." Nicholas Street also chided his auditors for their lapse into sinfulness. His sermon, *The American States Acting over the Part of the Children of Israel in the Wilderness,* observed that "the British ministry have been acting over the same wicked, mischievous plot against the American States, as Haman did against the Jews." Nevertheless, the Revolutionary War provided an unsurpassed opportunity for the people of God to take stock of themselves, "as God is thus pleased to bring his own people into a state of peculiar trials for the discovery of their virtues, so likewise for the discovery of their vices."

Victory over the British confirmed, at least in patriot eyes, America's special standing with God. Ezra Stiles in 1783 celebrated *The United States Elevated to Glory and Honour* while praising General Washington as the "American Joshua" and laying the groundwork for the Manifest Destiny of the next century. "It is probable that within a century of our independence," wrote Stiles, "the sun will shine on fifty million of inhabitants in the United States." Then, he continued, "The Lord shall have made his American Israel 'high above all nations which he hath made,' in numbers, 'and in praise, and in name, and in honour!' " Thomas Brockway echoed many of the same themes, including America's prerogative to push toward the Pacific, in *America Saved, or Divine Glory Displayed, in the Late War with Great Britain.* In 1788 Samuel Langdon's sermon, *The Republic of the Israelites as Example to the American States,* argued that "the sure way to be a prosperous and happy people" was for the new nation to institute the laws and polity of the Old Testament, a theme echoed in Abiel Abbot's *Traits of Resemblance in the People of the United States of America to Ancient Israel.*

Based in part on the solid rhetorical foundation of the colonial era, the notion of America's chosenness as a uniquely Christian land has persisted throughout the United States' entire history—to such a degree, in fact, that an extensive listing of examples would be more redundant than instructive. Some of the more diverse examples in this genre might include Thomas Jefferson's first, Abraham Lincoln's second, and John Kennedy's only inaugural addresses; Lyman Beecher's *Plan for the West,* Henry Ward Beecher's *Patriotic Addresses,* Samuel Baldwin's *Armageddon,* Washington Gladden's *The Nation and the Kingdom,* Ralph Barton Perry's *Our Side Is Right,* and Franklin Roosevelt's 1942 message to Congress. Even more recent pronouncements, such as Martin Luther King's "Letter from Birmingham Jail," while chiding Americans for their complacency, have also invoked the theme of America's chosenness.

The most significant development of the past decade, however, has been the emergence of conservative evangelicals as a political force. America, these Christians believe, has been mired for too long in self-doubt and recrimination following the Vietnam and Watergate debacles. It was time, they asserted, to stand up and "say something good about America." Abetted considerably by the historical interest arising from the Bicentennial, representatives of the so-called Christian Right began to produce books arguing with redoubled fervor the unique Christian origins and character of this nation.

Like others before them, the new Christian conservatives usually combine a celebration of America's Christian past with a condemnation of present-day moral decline, and then quickly turn to political prescriptions for redressing these ills. Some of these statements include *Listen, America!* and *Save America to Save the World* by fundamentalist preachers Jerry Falwell and James Robison respectively. Both invoke the notion of America's chosenness in laying out a conservative political agenda designed to call this country back to its religious roots. Jesse Helms, the New Right's denizen in Congress, added his own appeal, *"When Free Men Shall Stand."*

Convinced that American history can no longer be trusted to

"secular humanists," the Christian Right has provided its own version of the past in a number of textbooks. *Faith, Stars, and Stripes,* by Ronald Tonks and Charles Deweese, is a bicentennial contribution to this genre, while Rosalie Slater's *Teaching and Learning America's Christian History* represents an attempt to rewrite secondary-school instruction in conformity with the perceptions of the Christian Right. Peter Marshall and David Manuel's *The Light and the Glory* offers the same kind of interpretation of the divine origin and protection of America that the Puritan historian Thomas Prince had advanced in the eighteenth century.

Other contemporary writers have emphasized a strong relationship between Christianity and the founding of the nation, but at the same time do not hold to the Christian America idea per se. An example of this is the analysis of James Hitchcock, a Roman Catholic professor of history at St. Louis University, in *What Is Secular Humanism? Why Humanism Became Secular and How It Is Changing Our World.* This is probably the best discussion of the rise of secular humanism and the threat it poses to American culture today. Because the treatment is well-informed and balanced, its indictment of secular humanism is much more powerful than that found in most accounts. In a similar vein Francis Schaeffer's *A Christian Manifesto* calls for a direct confrontation with secular humanism in law and politics, and outlines a strategy for combating America's moral decline. John W. Whitehead's *The Second American Revolution* draws heavily on Schaeffer in his analysis, while calling for law to be bibliocentric.

STUDYING THE BELIEF IN CHRISTIAN ORIGINS

Historians in recent years have begun to take seriously America's consciousness of a Christian past. Some have noted the salutary effects of such a consciousness, while others recognize its liabilities. Most agree, however, that a belief in the uniquely Christian origins of this nation has deeply affected its character, its government, and its people.

Historians of the colonial period readily acknowledge the presence of millennialism as a motivating force in the consciousness of early settlers. J. F. Maclear's "New England and the Fifth Monarchy," for example, argues "that a preoccupation with the Last Things seems to have been a selective factor in drawing many eschatologically sensitive Puritans to the New World" and that the Puritans were utterly convinced they were "advancing history toward the day of Armageddon." James Davidson attempts to decipher *The Logic of Millennial Thought* in eighteenth-century New England. John Berens examines "the welter of religious-nationalist ideas articulated in post-1740 America" in his book *Providence and Patriotism in Early America*. Berens finds that for the patriots of the eighteenth century the "blessings of Providence distinguished the United States from other nations, illustrated America's singularness." Offering further evidence of the pervasiveness of religious consciousness in the Revolutionary era, Edmund Morgan's essay "The Puritan Ethic and the American Revolution" suggests that "the movement in all its phases, from resistance against Parliamentary taxation in the 1760s to the establishment of a national government and national policies in the 1790s was affected, not to say guided, by a set of values inherited from the age of Puritanism."

Many others have noted the profound influence of Puritanism on the American character, including Ralph Barton Perry in *Puritanism and Democracy*. Sacvan Bercovitch's *The Puritan Origins of the American Self* traces the influence of "Puritan themes, tensions, and literary strategies" on succeeding generations and notes the persistence of "the American self as the embodiment of a prophetic universal design." Bercovitch has made other important contributions in this field, including "The Typology of America's Mission," in which he states unequivocally that the "Puritans invented the sacred history of New England" and the "eighteenth-century clergy established the concept of America's mission." The emergence of a uniquely American typology is spelled out in greater detail in Bercovitch's *The American Jeremiad* and in Mason Lowance's *The Language of Canaan*. Both authors emphasize yet again the prevalence of Old Testament metaphors in the colonial period.

Works addressing the spiritual character of the new nation include Catherine Albanese's *Sons of the Fathers*, which records the emergence of a civil religion out of the Revolution, Mark Noll's *Christians in the American Revolution* ("a comparative study of religion and Revolutionary ideology in eighteenth-century America"), and Winthrop Hudson's "Theological Convictions and Democratic Government," which posits a more-than-coincidental connection between democracy and the Reformed tradition. Wesley Frank Craven's *The Legend of the Founding Fathers* surveys the various ways America's founders have been regarded through the years. In *This Sacred Trust* Paul Nagel, an intellectual historian, contends that a "persisting pattern of national consciousness" dominated nineteenth-century America, bequeathing to this century a "vaunted global responsibility and universal momentum." William Clebsch's article on "Christian Interpretations of the Civil War" illustrates the ability of theologians on either side of a dispute to argue their own sanctity while condemning the other side for its evil. James Moorhead's *American Apocalypse*, Timothy Weber's *Living in the Shadow of the Second Coming*, and Ernest Tuveson's *Redeemer Nation* demonstrate again the persistence of millenarianism as an interpretive framework for American self-consciousness.

A number of scholars have taken a broader view of the influence of religion throughout the whole of American history. Some of the studies falling into this category include H. Richard Niebuhr's *Kingdom of God in America*, Martin Marty's *Righteous Empire*, and Robert Handy's *A Christian America*. While Niebuhr assumes an essentially theological-historical approach to the issue, Marty offers a chronological history of what he calls the "Evangelical Empire" in America. And Handy takes on the difficult but critical task of assessing the differences between the lofty pronouncements and the realities of American religious life as American Protestants began gradually to regard the progress of civilization as a greater good than the Christianization of America. Winthrop Hudson's reader, *Nationalism and Religion in America*, addresses the question topically. In *Defining America*, Robert Benne and Philip Hefner provide an iconoclastic picture of Christianity in America and conclude that the "symbols of American identity" have combined to form a mythology which is "a betrayal of God and a falsification of the American experience."

The very complex but unmistakable interplay of religion and politics in America has caught the attention of Cushing Strout, Jerald Brauer, and J. F. Maclear, among many others. In *New Heavens and New Earth*, Strout surveys American history and comments on the "power of American culture to shape religion to its own ends." Brauer's "Rule of the Saints in American Politics" and Maclear's " 'True American Union' " both trace the persistence of religious influences on the political sphere back to the theocracy of the Puritans in New England. The legacy of the Puritan theocratic ideal was the conviction, in Brauer's words, that "God's will for America was eventually his will for the human race." Two of the many works addressing the relation of church and state in America are *Religion and the Republic,* edited by Elwyn A. Smith, and Mark DeWolfe Howe's excellent study *The Garden and the Wilderness.*

But, as Sidney Mead and others have observed, when religion is carried into the political sphere, compromise inevitably follows. His *Nation with the Soul of a Church* examines the "unresolved tension between the theology that legitimates the constitutional structure of the Republic and that generally professed and taught in a majority of the religious denominations of the United States." When Robert Bellah surveyed the national scene in 1967, he found "that there actually exists alongside of and rather clearly differentiated from the churches an elaborate and well-institutionalized civil religion in America." Bellah touched off a massive and continuing debate about the existence of an American civil religion. He quickly translated his discovery into his own jeremiad, arguing that civil religion "has often been used and is being used today as a cloak for petty interests and ugly passions," an argument elaborated in *The Broken Covenant.* The debate continues. A collection of essays called *American Civil Religion,* edited by Russell Richey and Donald Jones, approaches the controversy from a variety of perspectives. Robert Linder and Richard Pierard bring an evangelical slant to bear on the issue in *Twilight of the Saints: Biblical Christianity and Civil Religion in America.* Perry C. Cotham's *Politics, Americanism, and Christianity* looks at related questions from a singularly useful perspective, for Cotham is both an academically-trained political scientist and a minister in the Restorationist tradition. As such, he both appreciates the longing to "get back" to more Christian times, but is also aware of the dangers in that longing. And John F. Wilson's *Public Religion in American Culture* suggests that the civil religion proposal, actually "the advocacy of a religion of the republic," should be seen "as the attempt, through a variety of particular forms, to distill the old political culture of the United States which was supported by a broadly Protestant establishment." As such, the emergence of a civil or public religion serves as a revitalization effort in a society whose traditional values are threatened.

A vast number of works have recently appeared on the "New

Christian Right," many of them merely pot-boilers. By way of contrast, a sound general overview of the political actions and views taken by theological conservative Protestants in recent years, including those of the political conservatives, is Robert Booth Fowler's *A New Engagement: Evangelical Political Thought, 1966-1976.* A comprehensive bibliography by Richard V. Pierard, "The New Religious Right: A Formidable Force in American Politics," is a fine starting-point for studying the modern combination of theological and political conservatism. Gabriel Fackre, in *The Religious Right and the Christian Faith,* offers a more critical theological treatment of recent Christian conservatives. He argues that representatives of this perspective are deficient in their grasp of the faith. According to Fackre, such leaders, even when proclaiming their Christian intentions, give evidence of being deeply influenced by the very Enlightenment "humanism" they attack. From the other side of the issue, the book by Harold O. J. Brown, *The Reconstruction of the Republic,* is a forceful rationale for the urgency of the conservative position which makes full use of sophisticated theological categories.

EXAMINING THE EVENTS OF AMERICAN HISTORY

Another way to approach the question of America's Christian character is to step back from the belief that the nation is especially chosen in order to examine the actual events of American history themselves. Do these reflect a biblical approach to life? Do they meet God's standards for virtue? Those who attempt this approach do well to begin with a good textbook. Two of the finest, both coauthored by leading authorities, are *The National Experience: A History of the United States,* published by Harcourt, Brace, Jovanovich, and *The Great Republic: A History of the American People,* from D. C. Heath. This same approach can also benefit from an examination of the actual documents that have come from the crucial events of our history. Fine collections of such sources have been made available by Henry Steele Commager (*Documents of American History*) and Daniel Boorstin (*An American Primer*) for general American history, and by Edwin S. Gaustad (*A Documentary History of Religion in America*) for the story of America's Christians. Soon, however, the person who is interested in this question must turn to studies of some of the particular issues and events.

Of all the evangelical assumptions concerning America's past, none has been more enduring through the years than the view that the New World's earliest settlers migrated for religious reasons. To a degree at least, this is true, especially among the Pilgrims and Puritans of New England (see Perry Miller's "Errand into the Wilderness"). But such a sweeping generalization fails to account for the broad diversity of cultures that sprouted on the western shores of the Atlantic in the seventeenth century.

The first colonizers were Spaniards, and, as J. H. Parry establishes in *The Spanish Seaborne Empire,* their motives could hardly be characterized as religious. Spanish conquistadors fairly decimated the native population through disease or outright massacre in their quest for pecuniary gain. Although the Caribbean was the first theater for Spanish and English commercial expansion (Richard B. Sheridan, *Sugar and Slavery,* Richard S. Dunn, *Sugar and Slaves*), economic considerations prompted the founding of other Atlantic colonies as well. From its inception the Virginia Company sought profits in the New World, a point made emphatically in the early chapters of Wesley Frank Craven's *Dissolution of the Virginia Company.* Similar motives guided proprietors in the South (Converse D. Clowse, *Economic Beginnings in Colonial South Carolina*), and Frederick B. Tolles concludes in *Meeting House and Counting House* that many Quakers in Pennsylvania eagerly sought financial advancement. The Dutch established a formidable trading empire in New York (Thomas J. Condon, *New York Beginnings*). Within a generation even the godly Puritans had lost sight of the founders' zeal. Spiritual declension set in and, as Bernard Bailyn argues in *The New England Merchants in the Seventeenth Century,* mercantile interests began seriously to contend for control of the colony.

The influence of economic forces on American history extended well beyond colonization. Many historians, among them Michael Kammen in *Empire and Interest* and William Appleman Williams in "The Age of Mercantilism," conclude that economic self-interest lay behind both England's eighteenth-century colonial policies and the colonists' resolve to resist British imperialism. The potential of the American Revolution itself, perceived in terms of liberty and equality, was negated, many historians believe, by the Constitution and the shape of the new nation. Whereas the Revolution had been a radical movement, the Constitution was inherently a conservative one, protecting the interests of the affluent in the New World. This interpretation, propounded by E. James Ferguson ("The Nationalists of 1781-1783 and the Economic Interpretation of the Constitution") and Charles Beard (*An Economic Interpretation of the Constitution of the United States* and *Economic Origins of Jeffersonian Democracy*), among others, has by no means been universally accepted by historians (see Forest McDonald, *We the People*). But the argument remains important enough to warrant consideration by those who look upon the Revolution as merely a struggle for justice and right. Finally, Bray Hammond's excellent study, *Banks and Politics in America from the Revolution to the Civil War*, notes the persistence of economic forces in the formative years of the republic.

William McLoughlin points out in *Revivals, Awakenings, and Reform* that Americans periodically have sought religious awakenings to purge their various ills. Indeed, modern Christians can look back with no small degree of satisfaction on the salutary influence of revivals at critical points in American history (see, for example, Timothy L. Smith's *Revivalism and Social Reform*). And yet religious fervor, like an expiring mainspring, eventually dies down or is directed toward other ends. The blazing fires of America's first transcolonial revival, the Great Awakening of the 1730s and 40s, ignited the kindling for the Revolution, according to Alan Heimert in his ambitious study, *Religion and the American Mind*. Heimert may very well have stretched his conclusions beyond the limits of his evidence, as his critics charge, but Nathan Hatch handles the question of the relation between the Awakening and the Revolution more adroitly in *The Sacred Cause of Liberty*, and for this reason his assertion that the millennial rhetoric rising out of the Great Awakening evolved into a republican ideology is more convincing.

The First Awakening may have abetted the Revolutionary cause. But the Second Great Awakening did little to halt the exploitation of the powerless whom white Americans encountered in their westward march. And it did not stem the practice of slavery. There were exceptions, of course, but the reforming zeal of these revivals turned to issues such as temperance (Joseph Gusfield, *Symbolic Crusade*) more often than to abolition or demands for a humane Indian policy. This is not a trifling concern, for this country's treatment of blacks and Native Americans remains an unsightly scar.

As Henry Warner Bowden establishes in *American Indians and*

Christian Missions, successive waves of European colonizers approached the Indians differently, but generally agreed that the "savages" needed to be Christianized. Although he may not adequately account for millenarian motives, Neal Salisbury's portrayal of Puritan missions to the Indians, "Red Puritans," offers a picture that is simultaneously comic and pathetic. John Eliot, "apostle" to the Indians, segregated his charges into "praying towns," established a government modeled on the Old Testament, proscribed gambling, forbade males to let their hair grow long, taught them European formal logic, and dressed them in English-style clothing. The larger point of Salisbury's work is that conversion to Christianity more often than not entailed a conversion to European manners. Yet, converted or not, the Indian rarely was assimilated into the white man's culture. When the Indians could no longer tolerate encroachments on their territory and rose up in armed resistance, the white man used these uprisings to justify an unrestrained violence against the "savages" which amounted nearly to genocide.

Several historians have taken up the theme of white bellicosity toward the Indians. In *Regeneration through Violence,* Richard Slotkin sees it as part of a recurrent pattern throughout America's frontier history, while Francis Jennings in *The Invasion of America* views Puritan violence as simply another manifestation of their determination to conquer and subjugate the culturally inferior Indian. The white man's ignoble treatment of the Indian continued well past the colonial period. Reginald Horsman's "American Indian Policy in the Old Northwest" outlines the rapacious policies of the new nation, and Dee Brown's brilliant study *Bury My Heart at Wounded Knee* traces Manifest Destiny's relentless and fatal pursuit of the American Indian in the nineteenth century.

The history of the black man in America is even less inspiring. Crammed into slave ships and sold by the lot, the sweat of their brows produced some measure of prosperity for their owners while consigning the slaves themselves and their children to perpetual servitude. There is no tale more grisly in America's past. Winthrop Jordan's *White over Black* remains the best history of slavery from the colonial through the early national period. In "Slavery and Freedom: The American Paradox" and *American Slavery, American Freedom,* Edmund Morgan sets out to solve the great conundrum of American history: How can the nation which so vigorously laid claim to egalitarian and democratic principles be simultaneously the land of chattel slavery, the very antithesis of freedom? Looking at colonial Virginia, Morgan concludes that the introduction of slavery coincided with an attempt on the part of wealthy landowners to quell dissent within the white community, especially among white indentured servants. By instituting slavery and fomenting a fear and hatred of blacks, the white community—both landed and non-landed—united against a common black enemy.

Those who trumpet America's religious origins generally applaud the Christianity of the founding fathers. American blacks, however, might be pardoned for questioning the founders' morality. William Freehling in "The Founding Fathers and Slavery" surveys the rather specious attitudes of Jefferson and other founders. He credits Jefferson with restraining slavery by confining it to the South, but argues that Jefferson valued the union of the new nation infinitely more than abolition.

White Christians did indeed bring Christianity to their black chattels (Timothy Smith, "Slavery and Theology"), although the Bible lessons they gave to the slaves usually stressed obedience and submission rather than the biblical gospel of freedom in Christ. In an interesting counterpoint to Puritan consciousness of being the New Israel, Albert Raboteau points out in *Slave Religion* that blacks in this "Christian" country also appropriated the Old Testament flight from Egypt as a metaphor to describe their eventual deliverance from slavery to the Promised Land. Finally, lest anyone think that the Emancipation Proclamation ended forever the black man's search for justice and equality, it is only necessary to ponder the continuing struggle for legal parity since the 1960s, or consult accounts such as Dan Carter's riveting chronicle, *Scottsboro: A Tragedy of the American South*. The gloss of America's Christian morality begins to dim when works such as these are considered.

America's conduct of her wars is also a matter for serious Christian concern. Roland Bainton's *Christian Attitudes Toward War and Peace* sets the issue in a historic Christian context, while also providing some information on American events, which are the subject more directly of Edward LeRoy Long's *War and Conscience in America*. A massive study by Peter Brock, *Pacifism in the United States*, demonstrates the persistent fidelity of those religious groups, largely Christian and largely committed to Scripture, who have called into question the justice of warfare itself. A series of essays on America's major conflicts edited by Ronald A. Wells, *The Wars of America: Christian Views,* provides thought-provoking evaluations from the perspective of those who believe in the possibility of just wars. This book, which casts at least some doubt on the justice of most of the armed conflicts in our history, sets a very high standard for both solid history and solid Christian reflection.

Finally, some citizens regard this country as entirely too Christian—and not in any ethical sense. America's Jews have often found their Christian brethren to be lacking in charity, as indicated by Ruth Gay's *Jews in America* and "Some of My Best Friends" by Benjamin Epstein and Arnold Forster. In "Secular Society? A Jewish Perspective," Milton Himmelfarb contends that modern Jews have three choices ("to be Jews, to be Christians, to be secularists") and that from the "perspective of Jewish experience and of contemporary Jewish reality, the Western secular society is Christian as well as secular—and that includes America." Catholics, on the other hand, learned that Christianity in America usually meant Protestantism. Furthermore, as David Brion Davis ("Some Themes of Countersubversion"), Ray Billington (*Protestant Crusade*), and Donald Kinzer (*An Episode in Anti-Catholicism*) establish, American Protestants have resisted quite vigorously the advances of Catholics in America.

RESOURCES FOR CURRENT ACTION

A Christian who wishes to exert a positive influence on public affairs, but from the basis of a realistic picture of America, has a large number of resources to turn to. It is possible here to mention only a few of them, but the interested person will find extensive bibliographies readily available in many of these works and from other sources.

Good orientations to Christian participation in the modern political process are offered by Stephen Monsma, *The Unraveling of America,* and by Paul Henry, *Politics for Evangelicals.* Monsma's book discusses, as its subtitle puts it, "the inadequacies of current political options"—especially those classed as "liberal" and "conservative"—and it offers a self-consciously "Christian approach to government." Henry's book is a down-to-earth guide directed specifically to reactions which evangelicals often have to the political process. Both authors know what they are talking about, for they have each taught political science in Christian colleges and have served as representatives in state legislatures. A stimulating manual, with specific suggestions for grass-roots political discussion and participation, has been prepared by James Skillen in his capacity as executive director of the Association for Public Justice, *Christians Organizing for Political Service: A Study Guide Based on the Work of the Association for Public Justice*. The reflections of Mark Hatfield, *Between a Rock and a Hard Place*, on the possibilities and temptations of power which he has encountered as a member of the United States Senate, provide a moving personal account of one Christian's attempt to deal with the great public issues of the day.

Thought-provoking supplements to these basic books are offered by John Howard Yoder, *The Politics of Jesus*, Richard Mouw, *Politics and the Biblical Drama*, and Richard J. Neuhaus, *Christian Faith and Public Policies*. Yoder presents a strong biblical case for a consistently nonviolent approach to modern problems, especially those disagreements which lead to war. Believers, he holds, are to be engaged in no struggle on earth except for the cause of Christ, and then only with "weapons" of peace. Mouw grants with Yoder that Christians who resort to military and other forms of legitimated violence have done grave harm to the witness of the church. But he also maintains that God has given his people a mandate to rule the earth which allows for a cautious and humble use of restraint. Neuhaus has fewer doubts about the appropriate use of force, but his main concern is to argue for a realistically Christian assessment of both human nature and the world's self-serving character as a basis for responsible political action. A similar view is presented by Reinhold Niebuhr in his classic study *Moral Man and Immoral Society*. Niebuhr argues against naive optimism on the level of nations dealing with other nations. For Niebuhr the path to social justice in international relationships is not through idealistic compromise and accommodation. Rather, conflict is inevitable and power must be confronted by power.

The books by Yoder, Mouw, and Neuhaus treat the general biblical considerations which should guide Christian attitudes toward warfare. Other works, like Paul Ramsey's *The Just War*, move from general principles to concrete ethical dilemmas. Robert Clouse has edited a useful symposium, *War: Four Christian Views,* in which different authors present cases for nonresistance, pacifism, the just war, and preventive wars—each with a full attention to main principles of the Christian faith. Arthur Holmes, in *War and Christian Ethics,* presents a broad selection of readings to help in the shaping of responses to this vital issue. From Britain, Oliver O'Donovan's *In Pursuit of a Christian View of War* offers suggestions valuable also for Christians in the United States. Of many books on the question of nuclear warfare, Dale Aukerman's *Darkening Valley* is among the most profoundly rooted in the message of Scripture, and Ronald Sider and Richard Taylor's *Nuclear Holocaust and Christian Hope* focuses the question most sharply for evangelicals.

On a related issue, foreign policy, Ronald Kirkemo's *Between the Eagle and the Dove* is a sensitive primer on how a Christian may evaluate a government's international activity. John C. Bennett and Harvey Seifert carry the same discussion into a more profound consideration of theological standards in *U. S. Foreign Policy and Christian Ethics.* Some of the specific issues which these books address are now dated, but they still provide useful guidelines for Christian involvement in the considerations of foreign policy.

A very important question for modern American Christians concerns the issue of "lifestyle," since we live in a country which has prided itself on its affluence, its encouragement of individual acquisition, and its position of strength in the world. The books which address this issue often subject general perceptions of American traditions to rigorous Christian examination. In so doing they provide useful insights aimed at the application of biblical values to our current situation.

Francis Schaeffer pioneered with this sort of writing among evangelicals. *The Church at the End of the Twentieth Century* is a representative example of his challenge to North American Christians not to be captured by the materialistic values of modern America. Ronald Sider, who wrote *Rich Christians in an Age of Hunger* and who edited the collection, *Lifestyle in the Eighties: An Evangelical Commitment to Simple Lifestyle,* marks out the steps to an even sharper break with American traditions. To Sider, the believer is to be an example of self-giving charity and with fellow believers is to build a community devoted to the spread of the gospel and the promotion of justice. Two other books which make strong appeals for truly Christian living in modern America are *The Call to Conversion*, by Jim Wallis of the Sojourner community in Washington, D. C., and *Let Justice Roll Down*, by John Perkins of the Voice of Calvary Ministry in Mendenhall, Mississippi.

Christian reflection upon "lifestyle" in America must soon come to grips with the country's general political and economic traditions. Michael Novak, a fellow of the American Enterprise Institute and a Roman Catholic, has made a forceful case for the moral, and even Christian character of a free-enterprise system in his own book, *The Spirit of Democratic Capitalism*, and in books which he has edited for the Institute like *Democracy and Mediating Structures: A Theological Inquiry*. The perspective which Novak argues against is that which regards Western capitalism as an inherently predatory system from which the gospel provides liberation. A concise statement of this position, which is especially prominent among some sections of the Catholic Church in South America, is given by José Miguéz Bonino in *Doing Theology in a Revolutionary Situation*. The longer work by Gustavo Gutierrez, *A Theology of Liberation*, is an extensive rehearsal of similar themes. Both Bonino and Gutierrez attempt to synthesize Christian and Marxist perspectives, often by reformulating Christian theology in Marxist categories. The more general question of "revolutionary theology," and its implications for Christian life, is the subject of a discerning analysis from Andrew Kirk, *Liberation Theology: An Evangelical View from the Third World*. Kirk, who has lived in South America, sees the justice in much of the criticism of American-style capitalism, but has questions of his own concerning the radical proposals for Christian reform. Finally, Reinhold Niebuhr's *The Children of Light and the Children of Darkness: A Vindication of Democracy and a Critique of Its Traditional Defenses* remains a classic Christian evaluation of American political and economic traditions. Although it was published forty years ago, it still speaks forcefully to the strengths and weaknesses, the triumphs and ironies of "the American way."

Helpful resources for confronting the specific issues of the late twentieth century are also widely available. *Society, State, and Schools: A Case for Structural and Confessional Pluralism*, by Gordon Spykman and others, suggests sound Christian principles for sorting out relationships among government, Christian organizations, and the school systems. Another volume which shares some of the same perspective is *Disestablishment a Second Time* by Rockne McCarthy, James Skillen, and William Harper. This study offers an even more critical reading of American history on educational issues and more specific proposals for establishing "genuine pluralism for American schools." Two other recent books address specifically some of the questions which Christians have when beginning their own school systems or when seeking to work conscientiously in the public schools: David B. Cummings, ed., *The Basis for a Christian School*, and Cliff Schimmels, *How to Help Your Child Survive and Thrive in Public School*.

On the question of abortion, Franky Schaeffer's *A Time for Anger: The Myth of Neutrality* has pointed out the widespread biases of American media in reporting the issue. James T. Burtchaell's *Rachel Weeping: And Other Essays on Abortion* is only one of the many recent works providing both theoretical and practical suggestions for Christian response. A strong statement of the need for Christian action against world hunger, with specific guidelines on how to proceed, is *Bread for the World* by Arthur Simon. To mention just one more issue—the question of justice for prisoners, and how Christians may pursue it concretely, is the subject of the symposium edited by John Stott and Nicholas Miller, *Crime and the Responsible Community*, and of the popular autobiography by Charles Colson, *Life Sentence*.

★ ★ ★

The Christian task in modern America is complex. Without a wholehearted adherence to the authority of Scripture, without a full use of the church's internal resources, and without a realistic analysis of our contemporary situation, the job will not be done. The works mentioned in this last section suggest some ways to approach the task before us. This entire book is offered with the expectation that a clearer view of the past will contribute to that same goal.

SOURCES CITED

Abbot, Abiel. *Traits of Resemblance in the People of the United States of America to Ancient Israel* . . . Haverhill, MA, 1799.

Albanese, Catherine L. *Sons of the Fathers: The Civil Religion of the American Revolution*. Philadelphia, 1976.

Aukerman, Dale. *Darkening Valley: A Biblical Perspective on Nuclear War*. New York, 1981.

Bailyn, Bernard. *The New England Merchants in the Seventeenth Century*. Cambridge, MA, 1955.

Bainton, Ronald. *Christian Attitudes Toward War and Peace*. New York, 1960.

Baldwin, Samuel D. *Armageddon: or the . . . Existence of the United States Foretold in the Bible, its . . . expansion into the Millennial Republic, and Dominion over the Whole World . . .* Cincinnati, 1854.

Beard, Charles A. *An Economic Interpretation of the Constitution of the United States*. New York, 1914.

Beard, Charles A. *Economic Origins of Jeffersonian Democracy*. New York, 1915.

Beecher, Henry Ward. *Patriotic Addresses in America and England . . .* Edited by John R. Howard. Boston, 1887.

Beecher, Lyman A. *A Plea for the West*, second edition. Cincinnati, 1835.

Bellah, Robert N. *The Broken Covenant: American Civil Religion in Time of Trial*. New York, 1975.

Bellah, Robert N. "Civil Religion in America." *Daedalus: Journal of the American Academy of Arts and Sciences*, XCVI (1967), 1-21.

Benne, Robert, and Hefner, Philip. *Defining America: A Christian Critique of the American Dream*. Philadelphia, 1974.

Bennett, John C., and Seifert, Harvey. *U. S. Foreign Policy and Christian Ethics*. Philadelphia, 1977.

Bercovitch, Sacvan. *The American Jeremiad*. Madison, WI, 1978.

Bercovitch, Sacvan. *The Puritan Origins of the American Self*. New Haven, CT, 1975.

Bercovitch, Sacvan. "The Typology of America's Mission." *American Quarterly*, XXX (1978), 135-155.

Berens, John F. *Providence and Patriotism in Early America, 1640-1815*. Charlottesville, VA, 1978.

Billington, Ray A. *Protestant Crusade, 1800-1860: A Study in the Origins of American Nativism*. New York, 1938.

Bonino, José Miguéz. *Doing Theology in a Revolutionary Situation*. Philadelphia, 1975.

Boorstin, Daniel J., ed. *An American Primer*. New York and Chicago, 1969.

Bowden, Henry Warner. *American Indians and Christian Missions: Studies in Cultural Conflict.* Chicago, 1981.

Bradford, William. *Of Plymouth Plantation, 1620-1657.* Edited by Samuel Eliot Morison. New York, 1952.

Brauer, Jerald C. "The Rule of the Saints in American Politics." *Church History,* XXVII (1958), 240-255.

Brock, Peter. *Pacifism in the United States.* Princeton, 1968.

Brockway, Thomas. *America Saved, or Divine Glory Displayed, in the Late War with Great Britain.* Hartford, 1784.

Brown, Dee. *Bury My Heart at Wounded Knee: An Indian History of the American West.* New York, 1970.

Brown, Harold O. J. *The Reconstruction of the Republic.* New York, 1977.

Burtchaell, James T. *Rachel Weeping: And Other Essays on Abortion.* Fairway, KS, 1982.

Carter, Dan T. *Scottsboro: A Tragedy of the American South.* Baton Rouge, LA, 1969.

Checkley, Samuel. *The Duty of God's People when Engaged in War . . .* Boston, 1755.

Cherry, Conrad, ed. *God's New Israel: Religious Interpretations of American Destiny.* Englewood Cliffs, NJ, 1971.

Clebsch, William A. "Christian Interpretations of the Civil War." *Church History,* XXX (1961), 212-222.

Clouse, Robert. *War: Four Christian Views.* Downers Grove, IL, 1981.

Clowse, Converse D. *Economic Beginnings in Colonial South Carolina, 1670-1730.* Columbia, SC, 1971.

Colson, Charles W. *Life Sentence.* Old Tappan, NJ, 1981.

Commager, Henry Steele. *Documents of American History,* ninth edition. Englewood Cliffs, NJ, 1974.

Condon, Thomas J. *New York Beginnings: The Commercial Origins of New Netherland.* New York, 1968.

Cotham, Perry C. *Politics, Americanism, and Christianity.* Grand Rapids, 1976.

Craven, Wesley Frank. *Dissolution of the Virginia Company: The Failure of a Colonial Experiment.* New York, 1932.

Craven, Wesley Frank. *The Legend of the Founding Fathers.* New York, 1956.

Cummings, David B., ed. *The Basis for a Christian School.* Phillipsburg, NJ, 1982.

Davidson, James West. *The Logic of Millennial Thought: Eighteenth-Century New England.* New Haven, CT, 1977.

Davies, Samuel. *Religion and Patriotism, the Constituents of a Good Soldier.* Philadelphia, 1755.

Davies, Samuel. *The Curse of Cowardice: A Sermon Preached to the Militia of Hanover County, Virginia* . . . London, 1758.

Davis, David Brion. "Some Themes of Countersubversion: An Analysis of Anti-Masonic, Anti-Catholic, and Anti-Mormon Literature." *Mississippi Valley Historical Review,* XLVII (1960), 205-224.

Dunn, Richard S. *Sugar and Slaves: The Rise of the Planter Class in the English West Indies, 1624-1713.* Chapel Hill, NC, 1972.

Edwards, Jonathan. "The Latter-Day Glory is Probably to Begin in America." In Conrad Cherry, ed., *God's New Israel* [see full bibliographic citation above], pp. 55-59.

Epstein, Benjamin R., and Forster, Arnold. *"Some of My Best Friends . . ."* New York, 1962.

Fackre, Gabriel. *The Religious Right and the Christian Faith.* Grand Rapids, 1982.

Falwell, Jerry. *Listen, America!* New York, 1980.

Ferguson, E. James. "The Nationalists of 1781-1783 and the Economic Interpretation of the Constitution." *Journal of American History,* LVI (1969), 241-261.

Fowler, Robert Booth. *A New Engagement: Evangelical Political Thought, 1966-1976.* Grand Rapids, 1983.

Gaustad, Edwin S. *A Documentary History of Religion in America.* Grand Rapids, 1982-83.

Gay, Ruth. *Jews in America: A Short History.* New York, 1965.

Gladden, Washington. "The Nation and the Kingdom." In Cherry, ed., pp. 255-270.

The Great Republic, second edition. By Bernard Bailyn, *et al.* Boston, 1981.

Gusfield, Joseph R. *Symbolic Crusade: Status Politics and the American Temperance Movement.* Urbana, IL, 1963.

Gutierrez, Gustavo. *A Theology of Liberation.* Los Angeles, 1973.

Hammond, Bray. *Banks and Politics in America from the Revolution to the Civil War.* Princeton, NJ, 1957.

Handy, Robert T. *A Christian America: Protestant Hopes and Historical Realities.* New York, 1971.

Hatch, Nathan O. *The Sacred Cause of Liberty: Republican Thought and the Millennium in Revolutionary New England.* New Haven, CT, 1977.

Hatfield, Mark O. *Between a Rock and a Hard Place.* Waco, TX, 1977.

Heimert, Alan E. *Religion and the American Mind: From the Great Awakening to the Revolution.* Cambridge, MA, 1966.

Helms, Jesse. *"When Free Man Shall Stand."* Grand Rapids, 1976.

Henry, Paul. *Politics for Evangelicals.* Valley Forge, PA, 1974.

Himmelfarb, Milton. "Secular Society? A Jewish Perspective." *Daedalus: Journal of the American Academy of Arts and Sciences,* XCVI (1967), 220-236.

Hitchcock, James. *What Is Secular Humanism? Why Humanism Became Secular and How It Is Changing Our World.* Ann Arbor, 1982.

Holmes, Arthur F. *War and Christian Ethics.* Grand Rapids, 1975.

Horsman, Reginald. "American Indian Policy in the Old Northwest, 1783-1812." *William and Mary Quarterly,* 3d ser., XVIII (1961), 35-53.

Howe, Mark DeWolfe. *The Garden and the Wilderness: Religion and Government in American Constitutional History.* Chicago, 1965.

Hudson, Winthrop S. "Theological Connections and Democratic Government." *Theology Today,* X (1953), 230-239.

Hudson, Winthrop S., ed. *Nationalism and Religion in America: Concepts of American Identity and Mission.* New York, 1970.

Jennings, Francis. *The Invasion of America: Indians, Colonialism, and the Cant of Conquest.* Chapel Hill, NC, 1975.

Johnson, Edward. *Wonder-Working Providence of Sions Savior in New England.* Edited by J. Franklin Jameson. New York, 1910.

Jordan, Winthrop D. *White over Black: American Attitudes toward the Negro, 1550-1812.* Chapel Hill, NC, 1968.

Kammen, Michael. *Empire and Interest: The American Colonies and the Politics of Mercantilism.* Philadelphia, 1970.

Keteltas, Abraham. *God Arising and Pleading His People's Cause . . .* Newburyport, MA, 1777.

King, Martin Luther, Jr. "Letter from Birmingham Jail." In *Why We Can't Wait*. New York, 1963.

Kinzer, Donald L. *An Episode in Anti-Catholicism: The American Protective Association*. Seattle, 1964.

Kirk, Andrew J. *Liberation Theology: An Evangelical View from the Third World*. Richmond, VA, 1979.

Kirkemo, Ronald. *Between the Eagle and the Dove*. Downers Grove, IL, 1976.

Langdon, Samuel. *The Republic of the Israelites an Example to the American States*. Exeter, NH, 1788.

Linder, Robert D., and Pierard, Richard V. *Twilight of the Saints: Biblical Christianity and Civil Religion in America*. Downers Grove, IL, 1978.

Long, Edward LeRoy, Jr. *War and Conscience in America*. Philadelphia, 1968.

Lowance, Mason I. *The Language of Canaan: Metaphor and Symbol in New England from the Puritans to the Transcendentalists*. Cambridge, MA, 1980.

Lowell, John. *The Advantages of God's Presence with his People in an Expedition against their Enemies* . . . Boston, 1755.

Maclear, J. F. "New England and the Fifth Monarchy: The Quest for the Millennium in Early American Puritanism." *William and Mary Quarterly*, 3d ser., XXXII (1975), 223-260.

Maclear, James Fulton. " 'The True American Union' of the Church and the State: The Reconstruction of the Theocratic Tradition." *Church History*, XXVIII (1959), 41-62.

Marshall, Peter, and Manuel, David. *The Light and the Glory*. Old Tappan, NJ, 1977.

Marty, Martin E. *Righteous Empire: The Protestant Experience in America*. New York, 1970.

Mather, Cotton. *Magnalia Christi Americana, Books I and II*. Edited by Kenneth B. Murdock with Elizabeth W. Miller. Cambridge, MA, 1977.

McCarthy, Rockne M., Skillen, James W., and Harper, William A. *Disestablishment a Second Time: Genuine Pluralism for American Schools*. Washington, D.C., 1982.

McDonald, Forest. *We the People: The Economic Origins of the Constitution*. Chicago, 1958.

McLoughlin, William G. *Revivals, Awakenings, and Reforms: An Essay on Religion and Social Change in America, 1607-1977.* Chicago, 1978.

Mead, Sidney E. *The Nation with the Soul of a Church.* New York, 1975.

Miller, Perry. "Errand into the Wilderness." In *Errand into the Wilderness*, pp. 1-15. Cambridge, MA, 1956.

Monsma, Stephen. *The Unraveling of America: Wherein the Author Analyzes the Inadequacies of Current Political Options and Responds with a Christian Approach to Government.* Downers Grove, IL, 1974.

Moorhead, James H. *American Apocalypse: Yankee Protestants and the Civil War, 1860-1869.* New Haven, CT, 1978.

Morgan, Edmund S. *American Slavery, American Freedom: The Ordeal of Colonial Virginia.* New York, 1975.

Morgan, Edmund S. "Slavery and Freedom: The American Paradox." *Journal of American History,* LIX (1972), 5-29.

Morgan, Edmund S. "The Puritan Ethic and the American Revolution." *William and Mary Quarterly,* 3d ser., XXIV (1967), 3-43.

Mouw, Richard J. *Politics and the Biblical Drama.* Grand Rapids, 1976.

Nagel, Paul C. *This Sacred Trust: American Nationality, 1798-1898.* New York, 1971.

The National Experience, A History of the United States, fifth edition. By John Blum, *et al.* New York, 1981.

Neuhaus, Richard John. *Christian Faith and Public Policies: Thinking and Acting in the Courage of Uncertainty.* Minneapolis, 1977.

Niebuhr, H. Richard. *The Kingdom of God in America.* New York, 1937.

Niebuhr, Reinhold. *The Children of Light and the Children of Darkness: A Vindication of Democracy and a Critique of Its Traditional Defenses.* New York, 1944.

Niebuhr, Reinhold. *Moral Man and Immoral Society.* New York, 1932.

Niles, Samuel. *A Brief and Plain Essay on God's Wonderworking Providence for New-England . . .* New London, CT, 1747.

Noll, Mark A. *Christians in the American Revolution.* Grand Rapids, 1977.

Novak, Michael. *The Spirit of Democratic Capitalism.* New York, 1982.

Novak, Michael, ed. *Democracy and Mediating Structures: A Theological Inquiry.* Washington, D.C., 1980.

Noyes, Nicholas. *New-Englands Duty and Interest, to be an Habitation of Justice and Mountain of Holiness.* Boston, 1698.

O'Donovan, Oliver. *In Pursuit of a Christian View of War.* Bramcote, Nottinghamshire, England, 1977.

Parry, J. H. *The Spanish Seaborne Empire.* London, 1966.

Perkins, John. *Let Justice Roll Down.* Ventura, CA, 1976.

Perry, Ralph Barton. *Our Side Is Right.* Cambridge, MA, 1942.

Perry, Ralph Barton. *Puritanism and Democracy.* New York, 1944.

Pierard, Richard V. "The New Religious Right: A Formidable Force in American Politics." *Choice,* March 1982, 863-879.

Prince, Thomas. *A Chronological History of New England in the Form of Annals . . .* Boston, 1736.

Raboteau, Albert J. *Slave Religion: The "Invisible Institution" in the Antebellum South.* New York, 1978.

Ramsey, Paul. *The Just War: Force and Political Responsibility.* New York, 1968.

Richey, Russell E., and Jones, Donald G., eds. *American Civil Religion.* New York, 1974.

Robison, James, with Cox, Jim. *Save America to Save the World: A Christian's Practical Guide for Stopping the Tidal Wave of Moral, Political, and Economic Destruction in America.* Wheaton, IL, 1980.

Roosevelt, Franklin D. "Annual Message to Congress." In Cherry, ed., pp. 295-302.

Schaeffer, Francis A. *A Christian Manifesto.* Westchester, IL, 1981.

Schaeffer, Francis A. *The Church at the End of the Twentieth Century.* Downers Grove, IL, 1970.

Schaeffer, Franky. *A Time for Anger: The Myth of Neutrality.* Westchester, IL, 1982.

Schimmels, Clif. *How to Help Your Child Survive and Thrive in Public School.* Old Tappan, NJ, 1982.

Sheridan, Richard B. *Sugar and Slavery: An Economic History of the British West Indies, 1623-1775.* Baltimore, 1974.

Sherwood, Samuel. *The Church's Flight into the Wilderness.* New York, 1776.

Sider, Ronald J. *Rich Christians in an Age of Hunger.* Downers Grove, IL, 1977.

Sider, Ronald J., ed. *Lifestyle in the Eighties: An Evangelical Commitment to Simple Lifestyle.* Philadelphia, 1982.

Sider, Ronald J., and Taylor, Richard K. *Nuclear Holocaust and Christian Hope.* Downers Grove, IL, 1982.

Simon, Arthur. *Bread for the World.* Grand Rapids, 1975.

Skillen, James W. *Christians Organizing for Political Service: A Study Guide Based on the Work of the Association for Public Justice.* Washington, D.C., 1982.

Slater, Rosalie J. *Teaching and Learning America's Christian History: A Christian Education Guide for the American Christian Home, the American Christian Church, the American Christian School.* San Francisco, 1965.

Slotkin, Richard. *Regeneration through Violence: The Mythology of the American Frontier, 1600-1860.* Middletown, CT, 1973.

Smith, Elwyn A., ed. *The Religion of the Republic.* Philadelphia, 1971.

Smith, Timothy L. *Revivalism and Social Reform: American Protestantism on the Eve of the Civil War.* Gloucester, MA, 1976.

Smith, Timothy L. "Slavery and Theology: The Emergence of a Black Christian Consciousness in Nineteenth-Century America." *Church History,* XLI (1972), 497-512.

Spykman, Gordon, *et al. Society, State, and Schools: A Case for Structural and Confessional Pluralism.* Grand Rapids, 1981.

Stiles, Ezra. *The United States Elevated to Glory and Honour,* second edition. Worcester, MA, 1785.

Stott, John, and Miller, Nicholas, eds. *Crime and the Responsible Community.* Grand Rapids, 1980.

Street, Nicholas. *The American States Acting over the Part of the Children of Israel in the Wilderness . . .* New Haven, CT, 1777.

Strong, Cyprian. *God's Care of the New-England Colonies . . .* Hartford, 1777.

Strout, Cushing. *The New Heavens and New Earth: Political Religion in America.* New York, 1974.

Tocqueville, Alexis de. *Democracy in America.* Edited by Phillips Bradley. New York, 1946.

Tolles, Frederick B. *Meeting House and Counting House: The Quaker Merchants of Colonial Philadelphia, 1682-1763*. Chapel Hill, NC, 1948.

Tonks, A. Ronald, and Deweese, Charles W. *Faith, Stars, and Stripes: The Impact of Christianity on the Life History of America*. Nashville, 1976.

Tuveson, Ernest Lee. *Redeemer Nation: The Idea of America's Millennial Role*. Chicago, 1968.

Wallis, Jim. *Call to Conversion*. San Francisco, 1981.

Weber, Timothy P. *Living in the Shadow of the Second Coming: American Premillennialism 1875-1925*. New York, 1979.

Wells, Ronald A., ed. *The Wars of America: Christian Views*. Grand Rapids, 1982.

Whitaker, Alexander. *Good Newes from Virginia*. London, 1613.

Whitehead, John W. *The Second American Revolution*. Elgin, IL, 1982.

Wigglesworth, Michael. *God's Controversy with New England*. In *Proceedings of the Massachusetts Historical Society*, XII (1871-1873), 83-93.

Williams, William Appleman. "The Age of Mercantilism, 1763-1828." *William and Mary Quarterly*, 3d ser., XV (1958), 419-437.

Wilson, John F. *Public Religion in American Culture*. Philadelphia, 1979.

Winthrop, John. *A Modell of Christian Charity*. In Cherry, ed., pp. 39-43.

Yoder, John Howard. *The Politics of Jesus*. Grand Rapids, 1972.

Index

Please use also the Table of Contents as a guide to the themes of the book.